Naming the Violence

Naming the Violence

Speaking Out About Lesbian Battering

Edited by Kerry Lobel
for the National Coalition
Against Domestic Violence
Lesbian Task Force

The Seal Press

Published by The Seal Press, P.O. Box 13, Seattle, Washington 98111.

Publication of this book was made possible in part with assistance from the Chicago Resource Foundation.

Cover design by Laurie Becharas
Text design by Faith Conlon and Laurie Becharas

"'What Did He Hit You With?' The Doctor Said" by Chrystos was first published in *Sinister Wisdom*, Fall 1980. Reprinted by permission.

"Love is Not Enough" by Susan Crall first appeared under the title "Lesbian Violence: A Personal Account" in *Sisterlode*, November/ December 1984. Reprinted by permission.

"Love as Addiction: A Story of Battering" by Kate Hurley first appeared in *Common Lives, Lesbian Lives*, No. 8, Summer 1983. Reprinted by permission.

"Once Hitting Starts" by Lisa first appeared in *Coming Up!*, October 1984. Reprinted by permission.

Library of Congress Cataloging-in-Publication Data

Naming the violence.

    1. Abused lesbians—United States. 2. Lesbians—
United States—Psychology. I. Lobel, Kerry.
II. National Coalition Against Domestic Violence
(U.S.). Lesbian Task Force. III. Title: Lesbian
battering.
HQ75.6.U5N36   1986   306.7'663   86-15561
ISBN 0-931188-42-3

First edition, July 1986.

10 9 8 7 6 5 4 3 2 1

Acknowledgements

There are dozens of people without whom this book would not have been possible.

Mary Ann Snyder of the Chicago Resource Center and Sasha Hohri of the Ms. Foundation were early advocates for the book and were instrumental in obtaining funding for it from their respective foundations.

Barbara Smith from Kitchen Table: Women of Color Press offered much needed support and insight into the process of "doing" an anthology in the book's planning stages. Beth Richie, co-chair of NCADV's Women of Color Task Force, spent many hours talking with women of color about writing for the anthology and always had time for talk.

Lydia Walker wrote the grant without which funding for this anthology would not have been obtained. Beth Lightbown patiently typed and retyped many revisions to the anthology's manuscript.

Del Martin, author of two pioneering works, *Lesbian/ Woman* and *Battered Wives,* and Susan Schechter, whose comprehensive visioning of the battered women's movement, *Women and Male Violence,* have provided opportunities for many women to speak out about their lives as well as provided inspiration and much personal support.

Cindy Chin, former co-chair of the NCADV Lesbian Task Force, advocated for the anthology with funders and at conferences and meetings across the country. Barbara Hart, a tireless advocate for the empowerment of battered women, has raised issues of concern to battered lesbians around the country and was, along with Suzanne Pharr, instrumental in planning NCADV's forum on lesbian battering from which the idea for this book initiated. And Suzanne, as co-chair of the NCADV Lesbian Task Force, has had a vision for the national organizing that needed to precede this book and for the work that will follow it. Her work on lesbian issues has been a source of strength and support.

Barbara Wilson and Faith Conlon made a commitment to publish the anthology sight unseen. Faith has been a patient and insightful editor.

The editing team, Maria Zavala, Linda Giddings, Marcia LaRose, and Linda Shaw, spent countless hours reviewing and discussing manuscripts and providing direction for the anthology. Members of the National Battered Lesbians Task Force provided much needed criticism of the book's focus.

And finally, and most importantly, the book's contributors took an enormous risk in putting their lives and their ideas on the line.

CONTENTS

Introduction 1
Kerry Lobel

Preface 9
Barbara Hart

PART 1

"What Did He Hit You With?" The Doctor Said 19
Chrystos

The Second Closet: Battered Lesbians 21
Donna J. Cecere

Love is Not Enough 32
Susan Crall

Once Hitting Starts 37
Lisa

Will It Never End? 41
Cedar Gentlewind

For Better Or Worse 48
Breeze

Love as Addiction 56
Kate Hurley

"The Perfect Couple" 62
Cory Dziggel

PART 2

Battered Women's Shelters and Work with
Battered Lesbians 73
Lydia Walker

Making Shelters Safe for Lesbians 77
Linda Geraci

Support Groups for Battered Lesbians........................... 80
Nomi Porat

Lesbian Abuse: The Process of the Lesbian Abuse
Issues Network (LAIN)... 88
*Ann Strach, Nan Jervey, Susan Jan Hornstein and
Nomi Porat*

Safe Space for Battered Lesbians.................................... 95
*Barbara Hart and the Pennsylvania Coalition Against
Domestic Violence*

Community Organizing: One Community's Approach... 98
*Sue Knollenberg, Brenda Douville and
Nancy Hammond*

Organizing Safe Space for Battered Lesbians:
A Community Based Program.. 103
Linda and Avreayl

PART 3

Letting out the Secret: Journal Entries, 1982-1984......... 113
Sarah

Coming Full Circle... 124
Jeanne Cormier

It Couldn't Happen To Me.. 131
Kim

Lesbian Abuse: The Story Lies Under Our Wounds...... 137
Susan Kresge

She Never Really Hit Me... 148
Blair Northwood

Nothing Is the Same Anymore... 155
Mary Lou Dietrich

The Healing Comes Slowly.. 163
Arlene Istar

PART 4

Lesbian Battering: An Examination............................ 173
Barbara Hart

Lesbian Victims and the Reluctance to Identify Abuse.. 190
Nancy Hammond

How Homophobia Affects Lesbians' Response to
Violence in Lesbian Relationships............................... 198
Mindy Benowitz

Two Workshops on Homophobia............................... 202
Suzanne Pharr

Resources 225
Contributor Notes 227
About the Editor 233

Naming the Violence

Introduction

This anthology is a tribute to those battered lesbians who told their stories over and over again, giving many of us our understandings about lesbian battering. It is a tribute to those lesbians who at great personal risk worked hard to move many of us through our denial about lesbian battering. And it is a tribute to those women, lesbians and non-lesbians alike, who across this country are mobilizing community resources to provide education and services to the lesbian community.

Naming the Violence: Speaking Out About Lesbian Battering is a book by and for battered lesbians and those who work to support their empowerment. It is only the first step in speaking out about a problem that has been ignored too long. By gathering together the stories of battered lesbians and some analysis and suggestions for community change, we hope we can begin to move our communities toward breaking the silence around this issue.

The book grew out of a meeting, held in September 1983, sponsored by the Lesbian Task Force of the National Coalition Against Domestic Violence (NCADV). Attended by over one hundred participants, the meeting was the first opportunity for many of us to discuss lesbian battering outside of the context of our local communities. The meeting set the tone for the work — and the controversies — that have since surfaced throughout the country.

Although the meeting was organized to discuss lesbian battering, there was much denial, reluctance, and confusion surrounding the discussion. Although several participants revealed that they were battered lesbians in the meeting's opening sessions, other women who had not been battered identified their own capacity for violence, sympathized with batterers, and disavowed their own potential for victimization.

At great personal risk several of the battered lesbians at the conference told their stories and demanded that batterers and their communities be held accountable for the violence. This testimony had a dramatic impact on the conference participants. It was the battered women's movement at its best, with survivors of violence giving direction and leadership to the presentation of issues that affected them. Community action plans were an outgrowth of the meeting, leading many participants to clarify their sense that services to battered lesbians must be given highest priority, with essential consideration being given to educating shelters and lesbian social services.

By the end of the meeting, participants came to a consensus on a strong statement that defined lesbian battering, that supported the empowerment of battered lesbians as a priority, and which challenged lesbian communities to hold batterers accountable for their violence. The statement encouraged those in the lesbian community who participated in s/m relationships to explore their relationships for evidence of coercion and control. The statement, when released, created a controversy around the country. Proponents of lesbian sadomasochism attacked the document's section on s/m relationships. Others challenged the paper's definitions of lesbian battering. Still others discounted the lesbian community's responsibility for holding the batterer accountable.

The most important decision which came out of that September 1983 meeting was the decision to collect and publish the stories of battered lesbians along with articles that explored community organizing strategies.

The realization that effective strategies for empowering battered lesbians and ending violence in lesbian communities could only come from *listening* to the experiences of battered lesbians prompted the book's emphasis on personal accounts. The reluctance of many lesbian communities to confront abuse and the difficulties with getting shelters for battered women to acknowledge and be accessible to battered lesbians led to this book — a guide for lesbians to examine their own relationships, a challenge for communities that want to be accountable for providing safe space for battered lesbians, and some suggestions for communities that want to begin to organize.

Early on, four women from the NCADV Lesbian Task Force courageously volunteered to select manuscripts and determine the anthology's direction. Marcia LaRose, currently the director for the Portland Women's Crisis Line in Portland, Oregon, has been active in the women's anti-violence movement for nine years. Marcia is a formerly battered woman, the mother of six adult children and six grandchildren. Linda F. Giddings is an Eastern Band Cherokee-Choctaw-Creole, differently abled Indian Rights activist who has been an organizer in the movement to end violence against women and children for thirteen years. An incest survivor and former battered woman, Linda has co-founded (with the help of her partner of eleven years and their children) two domestic violence/sexual assault programs including a safe home program for battered lesbians. Linda Shaw was a co-founder of a battered women's program in Pennsylvania in the 1970s, where she developed and led support groups for both lesbian and non-lesbian women. And Maria Zavala has been a bilingual, bicultural counselor and legal advocate for Womanshelter/Compañeras in Holyoke, Massachusetts for the last four years. The daughter of migrants from Puerto Rico, Maria is an incest survivor and formerly battered woman, and the mother of a son.

In January 1985, I was selected to act as editor of the anthology. I have been active in the battered women's movement since 1976. I have worked for two years as an advocate in a shelter for battered women and their children and was the Director of the Southern California Coalition on Battered Women for five years before moving to Little Rock,

Arkansas in 1984. My work as a consultant to women's organizations and social change organizations has enabled me to work with programs throughout the United States.

I have been responsible for soliciting manuscripts, conducting specialized outreach to target communities, and coordinating the activities of the editing team with the NCADV Lesbian Task Force. I made all contacts with contributors and worked closely with them to clarify and revise their stories and articles. I've also been responsible for editing the manuscripts and organizing them into this book.

Manuscripts were solicited nationwide, beginning in the fall of 1984 with calls for papers directed to members of the NCADV Lesbian Task Force and Caucus, NCADV steering committee representatives, and key gay and lesbian publications and organizations. In April 1985, an article on the anthology was published in the NCADV *Voice* and circulated to shelters, domestic violence projects and coalitions throughout the country.

Following a review of contributions received by the editing team at its meeting in May 1985, the contributions' deadline was again extended, enabling the editing team to do more specific outreach to women of color, rural women, and differently abled women. Calls for papers were sent to organizations and newspapers serving the target groups, women's bars, women's bookstores and craftstores, gay and lesbian newspapers, women's radio and cable TV shows, women's organizations, and to conferences and workshops across the country. In addition, calls for papers were sent to publishers of books by and for women.

More than eighty contributors responded. Contributions came from throughout the country. For every contribution that was actually submitted, there were four phone calls or letters of inquiry from lesbians seeking support services in their area or asking for more information. Not every woman felt safe enough to tell her story publicly, even anonymously, fearing reprisal from her batterer or exclusion from her community — a community often unwilling to provide support and safe space.

Our outreach efforts succeeded in making diverse

communities more aware of the issues of lesbian battering and the editing team more aware of the special problems of the battered women we were trying to reach. Many women of color and differently abled women were reluctant to discuss their experiences for publication in the anthology, calling the battered women's movement and lesbian communities to task for excluding them from services and leadership roles. Many women told of being stigmatized by their communities — communities which could not accept their sexual preference. We say this as a way to affirm that there are a great many stories to be told and many organizing strategies to be shared. We do not tell them all or share them all in this anthology, and for that we have many regrets.

The editing team's work lasted for over a year and a half. Meetings of the editing team were difficult ones. Discussing the powerful content of the manuscripts meant discussing and sorting out our feelings about our own relationships, past and present. Choosing manuscripts necessitated airing our own views about lesbian battering, services for battered lesbians, and services for abusers. While the team had many disagreements about approaches to services and strategies, the manuscripts in this book were included by consensus decision.

Recognizing that the safety and empowerment of battered lesbians must be a first priority, the editors of this anthology have made a conscientious effort to focus on the stories of battered lesbians and on community organizing strategies which support the empowerment of battered lesbians.

For many readers the stories will raise questions about the connections between violence and chemical dependency, childhood abuse, homophobia, and internalized homophobia. These questions must not divert our attention from the truths that emerge from the personal accounts — that emotional and physical violence are used as effective tools of power and control and that the abuser makes a choice about using violence. Only when the violence stops can these other issues be fully explored and resolved.

The anthology is divided into four sections. The first and third sections contain the stories of battered lesbians from throughout the country, chronicling their lives as battered women and as survivors of emotional and physical abuse. Anger, guilt, shame, confusion, and most of all *strength,* emerge as common themes from the personal accounts. The second and fourth sections of the anthology deal with community organizing activities. We have tried to focus these sections on activities that support the empowerment of battered lesbians. These include concrete strategies for ensuring communities that are committed to holding abusers accountable for their abuse, approaches for providing services to battered lesbians in shelters and support groups, and tools for doing homophobia and internalizing homophobia workshops. Three questions will be useful to communities evaluating their own work.

• Are battered lesbians and formerly battered lesbians involved in leadership roles in planning the activity?

• How does the activity contribute to the empowerment of battered lesbians?

• Have precautions been taken to assure the safety of battered lesbians?

This anthology is a moment of our history caught in time. As this book goes to press, organizing activities across the country continue to proliferate. The community work and the ideas presented in the anthology are only a small cross section of the activities taking place nationwide.

Any anthology of this kind is the product of a team effort. Hundreds of women from throughout the country have gathered in groups, large and small, over the last ten years to discuss the role of lesbians within the battered women's movement. Dozens of women have brought their experiences as battered lesbians to community forums, conferences and workshops. And hundreds of women, lesbians and non-lesbians alike, have initiated activities in their local communities. Each of these women's experiences have touched this book.

Publicly addressing the issue of lesbian battering, while necessary, is done with the recognition that we live in increasingly repressive times. The hard-won gains of the civil rights movement, women's movement and gay and lesbian rights movements over the past twenty-five years have been met by increasing resistance and setbacks. Many lesbians are understandably reluctant to air issues related to lesbian battering, for fear of triggering homophobic attacks on our communities. In a society where there has been no acceptance of lesbian relationships, these fears are legitimate.

By discussing these issues openly, we risk further repression. Yet, our only alternative is one of silence, a silence that traps battered lesbians into believing that they are alone and that there are no resources available to them. With this book, we are breaking that silence.

Kerry Lobel
April 1986

Preface

Barbara Hart

I have been waiting for this book for almost ten years. In the late fall of 1975, I came out for the second and final time. Shortly thereafter, I began to realize that there was violence in lesbian relationships. Women were beating and terrorizing other women. I was shocked and dismayed.

In the intervening years, I have tried to talk with the lesbian community about lesbian battering. This was sometimes a lonely and frustrating experience. More importantly, it has been a dangerous and desperate ten years for those lesbians who are victims of physical and sexual abuse inflicted by their partners.

The wall of silence surrounding lesbian battering has been virtually impenetrable, as has the wall of isolation, keeping lesbian victims separate from and unsupported by our community.

I believe that we have much to learn yet about violence in lesbian relationships. Clearly, we do not know how to confront it. We do not have a system internal to our community which permits us to hold lesbian batterers accountable. We have not yet created safe space for battered lesbians. We have much work yet to do.

However, any intervention will fail or further endanger battered lesbians unless it is one that is shaped by the experience of all battered lesbians and tailored to the specific needs of a lesbian victim. Therefore, we must listen to battered lesbians. This anthology is the beginning of that listening. The listening is painful. It challenges our dream of a lesbian utopia. It contradicts our belief in the inherent nonviolence of women. And the disclosure of violence by lesbians against lesbians may enhance the arsenal of homophobes, who seek to stifle the free and whole participation of lesbians in this society.

Yet, if we are to free ourselves, we must free our sisters. We must courageously stand with battered lesbians against those whose violence jeopardizes their very lives.

A first step for those of us who are not battered but are lesbians is to understand the experience of battered lesbians. After understanding will come clarity, courage, direction and vision.

Early Learning about Lesbian Battering

My process of understanding began soon after I came out in 1975. My lover and I began searching for a community of other lesbians outside of our small city. This search took us to many women's gatherings. Often there were group discussions about lesbian relationships. Frequently, these focused on alcoholism and sexual dysfunction as causes for troubled relationships. There were not even innuendoes of violence in these discussions, only the implications of very serious discord. We did not want to believe that there was violence. I did not apply the lessons I had learned as a woman battered in the early 70's to the kind of control and power issues about which we were hearing.

Our ignorance persisted despite the fact that we began to organize a shelter for battered women in conjunction with a group of straight women in our town. We were so clear about violence as a mechanism for control and domination of heterosexual women. We did not make the connection necessary to recognize the violence in lesbian relationships.

However, during my second year, my lover left to go to Boston and pursue a post-graduate degree. I became lonely, and knowing no other way of contacting lesbians, I began to go to the local gay bars. There seemed to be a script that violence was tolerated in bars. On almost every occasion that I went and stayed until closing, there was an episode of violence, sometimes very minor, but at other times very frightening. I began to conclude that violence was a ritual of "bar dykes" who acted out when they were at bars. I did not think of the violence being played out at home.

I saw a lot of property damage and public humiliation. Yet, I saw each assault as a discrete and independent incident. I had no sense that the victims of assault were terrorized and controlled as I had been as a battered woman.

Nonetheless, my naiveté and misconception soon ended. The week of New Year's, 1978, I sheltered a battered lesbian. As I listened to her story unfold, I heard how her partner had beaten up all of her women lovers since coming out. The community had done nothing. It never warned women about Kim. It never intervened to stop her violent rampages. It shunned the victim. It blamed the battered lesbian for the excruciating abuse imposed upon her.

It was at this time that I began to make connections between my experience as a battered woman and the experience of battered lesbians. I decided to extend myself to lesbian victims for support and safety planning. A number of dykes came to me for support and clarification. Often they had been deserted by friends, who seemingly avoided them because of their "weakness."

Soon I was asked to intervene to confront batterers legally — to confront the batterer — to name the violence, to demand a cessation of the violence and to insist that the batterer have no contact with the victim. In this capacity, I advised the batterer that the victim was prepared to follow through with civil or criminal prosecution absent voluntary compliance. In fact, I assisted one woman in obtaining a civil protection order against her lover.

However, the lesbian community was not pleased with this process of accountability. They preferred to believe that the violence only occurred on Saturday nights and was something that the community could contain.

First Gathering To Discuss Lesbian Battering

In January of 1978, the U.S. Commission on Civil Rights held a national hearing on women abuse in Washington, D.C. Thanks to the organizing and outreach efforts of Valle Jones, hundreds of advocates for battered women from around the country came to testify about violence in the lives of women. While some women testified, others began organizing what was to become the National Coalition Against Domestic Violence (NCADV).

Meanwhile, lesbians in the movement decided to meet together for support and problem-solving. Although there was some resistance from non-lesbian women, alleging that we were attempting to divide the group and discredit the movement, about forty courageous lesbians met in an empty ballroom. Two issues were repeatedly addressed by the group. One was homophobia in battered women's programs. The other was lesbian battering.

The revelations about lesbian abuse by and of our partners was shocking and frightening. Although we could not reach consensus about the causes or dimensions of lesbian violence, we quickly agreed that this discussion could not be taken to non-lesbian women in the movement. We felt it would destroy our credibility and that it would make us even more vulnerable to homophobic attacks by our sisters and those people in the dominant culture that wanted to discredit the efforts of the battered women's movement. So, we pulled a tight lid down on the subject and did not discuss lesbian battering even among ourselves until the first NCADV conference two years later. I was concerned that battered lesbians were being ignored, even sacrificed, to enable us to work on safer issues.

Workshops on Lesbian Battering

In 1981, I was asked to co-facilitate a workshop on homophobia and to lead a workshop on lesbian battering. The workshop on lesbian battering was open to non-lesbian as well as lesbian women by agreement of the participants. However, we asked that participants preserve the confidentiality of the discussion and of the identities of those women who decided to identify themselves as lesbians and speak about their experiences. The discussion was a very difficult, but careful and respectful one. Many again wanted to disclaim lesbian battering and to relegate it to bar dykes and butches. The group would not permit this denial.

We recognized how threatening the reality of lesbian battering was to our dream of lesbian utopia — a nonviolent, fairly androgynous, often separatist community struggling for social justice and freedom for ourselves and other oppressed people. Nonetheless, for many in the group, the dream was shattered by recognition of violence within our community. Many of us realized that we had been fooling ourselves by believing that we were close to or within reaching distance of that utopia. The recognition of violence informed us that we had a long, hard struggle ahead. By the end of the session, all women had reembraced the dream — some of us committed to confronting lesbian battering and others hopeful that this problem would quickly resolve itself.

NCADV Begins a Dialogue on Lesbian Battering

At the NCADV conference in Milwaukee in 1982, formerly battered lesbians demanded that the caucus deal with lesbian battering as a priority. Many voices joined with them. Some were asking the Lesbian Task Force of NCADV to deal with the sexual violence they experienced as survivors of sadomasochism.

Issues of homophobia within the movement and the task of organizing regional networks of lesbians and identifying a contact person in each region became the principle foci of caucus work at the national conference. However, the leadership of the Task Force agreed to sponsor a dialogue on lesbian battering in the near future.

This dialogue occurred in September of the following year. The dialogue taught me three important lessons.

1. As a lesbian community, we identify with the power, control and anger of lesbians who batter. We identify ourselves as potential batterers. We do not recognize that we risk being the targets of abuse in our relationships; that we deny our vulnerability; and that we are like battered women who stay in relationships with an abusive person despite the violence. We view lesbians who are battered as weak sisters. We must work to change this consciousness.

2. Although we listened to battered, non-lesbian women to understand women abuse, we are not anxious to listen to battered lesbians to understand lesbian violence. Instead, we prefer to superimpose our own beliefs about lesbian battering on survivors, denying their reality and asking them to fit into our vision of a battered lesbian—to be worthy of our support. We must change. We must listen to the voices of battered lesbians and recognize that their analysis and understanding of lesbian battering is correct. We must accept the leadership of battered lesbians.

3. Unless our communities are accountable to battered lesbians, they can never be safe or empowering for lesbian survivors.Therefore, we need to develop strategies to assure safety and to devise mechanisms for requiring accountability of batterers.

Although we agreed at the dialogue not to intervene and request accountability of any batterer unless we were asked to do so by a battered lesbian, and although we agreed to shape and limit our request for acountability to that which was asked by the battered lesbian, questions arise:

• Is there a larger accountability to other lesbians and to the battered women's movement to disclose the presence of lesbians among us who have not acknowledged their abuse and have not stopped patterns of violence or been accountable to the women they battered?

• Is service to battered lesbians enough?

• When can we trust the lesbian batterer?

• Must all lesbian victims move on to new communities to gain safety?

• Will we always be angry at lesbian survivors for breaking the silence that supports our dreams and visions of a united, nonviolent, celebratory lesbian community?

• Since some of us hold out real hope that batterers will change and eliminate their coercive and violent behaviors, and others of us have virtually no hope that batterers will give up the power and control that they gain or maintain over others by violence, what do we do about these differences while trying to develop a united community?

I have no answers other than for myself about these questions. Our movement and our communities must examine them and reach careful but prompt conclusions.

Even if the lesbian community cannot yet figure out effective and safe ways to confront batterers and does not know how to definitively prevent lesbian assaults or how to make our community safe for battered lesbians, I trust that we will work on solutions. Meanwhile, we do know how to provide services to battered women and we have a moral and political obligation to promptly see that adequate services are available to battered lesbians in our communities. We do not need to wait or further deliberate on how to provide services to battered lesbians. This is not to provide us with an excuse for avoiding these harder issues. It is to say that our first obligation is to provide safety and advocacy for lesbians abused in intimate relationships.

Moving On

I trust that this anthology will help each of us begin to form an analysis of violence against lesbians, as well as inspire us to provide quality services for our sisters and tackle the difficult issues of safe space for lesbian survivors in our movement, accountability for batterers and prevention of violence in ourselves and others.

Thank you NCADV, the Lesbian Task Force, Kerry Lobel and authors, for your courageous contributions. I trust that if NCADV creates another anthology in ten years, we will have many of the answers we are now seeking.

PART ONE

"What Did He Hit You With?" The Doctor Said

Chrystos

Shame. Silence.
Not he.
She.
I didn't correct him.
Curled into myself like a deformed foot
I looked at the floor
ceiling
evading.
A fist.
Hand that has spread me open
fingers I've taken inside me
Screaming I love you bitch
You are the she
who rocked my head side to side
barrier reef for your rage boat
It's safe to beat me
I've lain under your tongue
between your thighs
hungry
When I grabbed you to throw you off
you shouted, "If you've scarred my face
bitch
I'll kill you!" "I'm sorry," I wept, "I didn't mean to scratch
you."

Should have said you won't have a chance to kill me
I'm gonna kill you for thinking you can hit me like that
screaming that you love me
You said, "I haven't hit a woman in 8 years."
8 years bad luck my head caught it
My arms in dishwater scrubbing out my father's shoe
the dream tells me
you're familiar
that brutality I slide in without a horn
"You don't have to be beaten to be loved," the therapist said
I held the cool shock of those words
against the purple bruise of still wanting you
You've hit me with that irresistable
deadly weapon:
hatred dressed in the shoes and socks of the words
I love you

The Second Closet: Battered Lesbians

Donna J. Cecere

> *You feel like you are in a no-win situation.
> Damned if you do and damned if you don't.
> The tension between the two of you starts to
> build and you have already learned that noth-
> ing you do or say is going to make a difference.
> As they say: "You don't deserve it, but you're
> going to get it anyway."*

Your stomach hurts a lot these days.

> *It seems that nothing you do is good enough.
> You make the bed, only to have her take it apart
> and make it again. You map out a trip that the
> two of you have been planning, and she takes it
> to someone at AAA to do it over. You are not
> trusted with the simplest of tasks.*

You begin to feel worthless.

> *Except for occasional token atonements, your
> wants and needs seem to always come second.
> It is easier to give in to her demands than to go
> one more round. You find yourself agreeing
> when you want to disagree, swallowing your
> pride and sacrificing your personal integrity for*

21

> *the sake of keeping peace. You give in to prove
> your love.*

Physically and emotionally, you feel
exhausted.

*She accuses you of sleeping with other women
(and your male friends). You are expected to
account for all your time away from her. She is
jealous of your friendships and your family.
You feel set up to choose between her and your
friends, her and your children, her and your
work. You gradually isolate yourself from the
world to try to make her feel more secure and
more loved—and to avoid another fight.*

You feel you are suffocating.

*You know that she loves you, but when
something (anything!) out there angers her, she
takes it out on you. You try to compensate, try
to control the environment to keep her from
getting upset, but sometimes she walks in the
door that way. Maybe this time she'll just yell
some insults and blow off steam. Maybe she'll
throw you up against the wall or hit you. Maybe
she'll beat the hell out of you. Would she
actually kill you?*

You feel helpless, responsible and guilty.

I have to admit right off that I resisted even starting this
writing for a few reasons that I can identify: One: I feel a
lingering sense of embarrassment (self-blame/shame?) at
having been involved in a battering relationship, though it is
now five years, light years worth of personal counseling and
growth and countless hours of community-awareness
organizing later.

Two: There is still a touch of fear of retribution from my ex-
lover/batterer. From time to time I berate myself for being so
"paranoid," but I also know that in my life I generally do not

fear when there is no reason to fear. I no longer suffer nightmares of her trying to kill me. But the sound of her, voicing accusations into the phone, has been enough to make me careful about how I do my work, where I work, and whether or not I use my name. I still do not name her. But, today I learned of a fellow worker in our community who is presently being terrorized by his ex-lover/batterer. He, like me, continues his work, looking over his shoulder, and lives with the ever-present awareness that there is someone out there who has proven himself/herself a danger to our personal safety and well-being. I can't keep quiet.

The third reason I resist the task of this writing is that it obviously isn't the most pleasant thing to write about. I'm sitting here in Cheeseman Park watching people play, enjoying the first chance I've had this year to sit in the sun and watch the clouds and the kites in the sky. I count nine. Two grounded. It's just too beautiful a day to write about violence and fear.

Then again, I've been promising myself for five years now that I would put all of this down on paper — for the sake of setting the record straight, to help those in battering relationships to name their situations, and also because I still feel the need to tell my story.

We were together for two years. The abuse began early on, though I didn't know enough then to make such a connection. Though a Lesbian Feminist activist for years at that point, I still thought of battering as, first, a male-against-female act, and second, as being a physically violent act. I had no concept of what emotional, psychological and spiritual abuse was about.

Like many battered people, I didn't see it coming. And if I had had a sense about what lay ahead, I was far too ignorant to call it what it was. After all, we were in love and we were intelligent women of high political consciousness (whatever that means).

I need to clarify at this point, that the abuse I suffered was mostly verbal and emotional, which many battered people will testify as being the real event. You can be involved in a devastatingly brutal relationship, with all of the extreme emotional consequences, and never have a hand raised against you.

For myself, the physical outbreak of violence occurred infrequently, but I lived with the knowledge that the threat or possibility of physical violence could happen. I was often distracted from the real issue in our relationship and quieted by her reminders that the brutality suffered by her lovers previous to myself was far worse than anything I suffered, physically. I'm sure this is true, but the real message she was delivering (and which I bought) was that I didn't have anything to complain about since others had suffered more harm than I, and after all, she was trying to control herself.

I backed off.

I understood.

I forgave.

And I felt sorry for her.

I still feel sorry for her. Well, it's more like pity. She came from a home situation where she was the victim of what ranged from severe neglect to severe violence, which I later became convinced also included sexual abuse, though she would never betray her family by claiming such a thing.

She was so afraid and so tormented by her past. I listened and I held her through all the tears and the horror stories and the re-living of the terrifying and bloody nightmares she experienced so often.

I sometimes felt like I was taking care of a scared little girl while she told her stories with all intense emotions as though it were twenty-five minutes instead of twenty-five years that had passed since the actual event. She carried such a rage around inside of her. Part of me was paralyzed with fear of that rage and part of me wanted to relieve her of its burden and torture.

I loved her for her ability and willingness to survive a childhood filled with such trauma and pain, and I sympathized. We moved right into a way of relating in which it became my role in our relationship to *make up* for all that pain, all those terrifying times and denial of love. Clearly an unhealthy way of relating, but it wasn't clear to me at the beginning. I thought the strength of our love could heal all those old wounds.

And I felt for a long time that I had failed her.

We loved each other and I was taken with the apparent intensity of her feelings for me. I guess "dramatic" might be more accurate a term, but it was the first relationship for me in which the woman I was so in love with was also in love with me. I couldn't believe my fortune. There was all the specialness and passion I had ever wanted. She was striking and intelligent and always willing to take a stand. We opposed and fought sexism, racism and homophobia, with pride and conviction.

The stickler in our little paradise was a growing habit of condescension which I at first interpreted as a by-product of ageism (she was ten years older than I). She didn't seem to value my opinions much and had little trust in my intellect. My stories more amused than moved her and I became more and more hurt by it. I let it go and let it go until I could let it go no more. The next put-down was met with a challenge. I let her know that some of her attitudes towards me were insulting and I felt I deserved more respect.

From that came our first fight (a yelling match) in which she told me that if I was so insulted and felt that I was being treated so badly, I could leave. I took her apartment key off my key ring, left it on the bed and headed for the door. That's when the first incidence of violence occurred.

In the following two years, I tried to walk out on her many times; each time the attempt was met with physical violence or threats of suicide.

The physical abuse I endured ranged from pushing and being restrained against my will to slaps and a tackle which produced a back injury that left me in pain for several months. I never sought medical help, mostly out of fear of having to explain or lie about what had happened. My injuries were not visible, except perhaps in my mood. For many months I repeated to myself, "This is not happening." I knew *it was* and did not want to believe it. It was a very personal hell.

There was the time that she made a move to strangle me, and was shocked that I bothered to defend myself. And there was the time when she woke me in the middle of the night with her crying because she had awakened to find me sleeping so still that she imagined she must have killed me.

There were the tantrums and the dramatic mood swings. I was at a loss to try to find the rhyme or reason to what would set her off.

There was the time I had to talk her out of buying a gun, not out of any strong convictions on my part around gun control, but because I thought I had a pretty good idea who she might threaten with it. It was the only time in my life I've ever used the words "I forbid it!"

I allowed her to convince me that I was the one who instigated the abuse. It seems that any time my needs differed from hers, I was being abusive. If she wanted to go to the movies and I wanted to stay home and finish schoolwork, *that* was supposed to be abusive on my part. Fights erupted almost daily over these kinds of things, and I gradually came to see that for *her* this was normal. *Every* couple fights, right? But our conflicts were almost constant and I gradually lost weight (down to eighty-nine pounds, at one point), I was constantly exhausted and suffered from headaches and an ulcer condition. I developed several cysts and PID and was almost hospitalized for these lack-of-health conditions. In trying to relate to my best friend what was happening to my body (which for all of my life up to that point had been relatively free from illness) I realized that for the months that this condition was developing, my lover had repeated to me many times that I was going to die. Upon learning of this my best friend said, "For Christsakes, she's talking you into it! You've got to get away from it." Which I did for three days. Long enough to fast, do some soul-searching meditation/healing work and set into process a momentum to correct the conditions that had caused the deterioration of my health.

We were together only six months after that. I had told her at one point that I would no longer accept apologies from her, figuring that it was in part my forgiving of these acts that allowed her to turn around and repeat them. All I actually succeeded in doing was obliterating the only nice phase of our relationship — the "making-up" phase. Our relationship became a two-part cycle: tension-abuse, tension-abuse.

I remember thinking that the only way out, the only way to

change this situation was for one of us to die. I couldn't leave her because of the threats and also because I still loved and needed her. I was half convinced I'd never find love again and not so sure that I would want to after this anyway. But death came to seem the only way out and that thought scared me. I came to understand how battered people sometimes finally murder their batterers.

But I found another way out: I went to therapy. She left me two weeks later. After two years of the confusion of our relationship (How could someone who loves me treat me this way?), suffering accusations and always struggling to prove myself and my love and yet blaming myself, I was left emotionally and behaviorally paralyzed. I worked with an excellent counselor who had some experience counseling lesbians and some experience counseling battered women, but never a battered lesbian. We did good work together and with the patience and support of my close friends and an understanding family I set out to recover and to transform my pain into personal power. I worked through guilt and fear and my own outrage at what I had put up with. After all the self-doubt and self-blame, it was a powerful realization and an important step in self-affirmation to be able to say that it was not wrong of me to trust her. *It was wrong of her to betray my trust.*

Along with personal counseling I did the feminist thing and began to work on bringing the issue of battering in gay and lesbian relationships out of the closet. I hooked up and helped to form a group called RUTH, which was a support group for battered lesbians. Along with my friend Blair, I put on workshops, did interviews with the lesbian press, circulated information on how to determine if you are a battered person, spoke to mental health groups and shelter workers. We received phone calls from women all over the country, proof that our experience was not an isolated and unique problem.

As with many problems that we confront within our community, we translate the personal pain and fear into activity. We form support groups, organize conferences, set up hotlines, provide safe space and opportunities for learning, sharing and healing. We present our stories of horror and survival. We cry, we mourn, we get angry. We blame ouselves, we blame someone else and eventually work our way to the calm after the storm, pick up our pouch of learnings and move on. Some of us move on to other issues, working against other forms of assault on our people and our spirit, and carrying with us an awareness and a reclaiming of the right and the ability and the courage to love, and to no longer live in fear. We laugh again.

For me, the real crime, the real sin in battering is the fear it strikes in a person's heart. Anything that makes you afraid is an act against your spirit, for when you are afraid, you don't really live.

I resent the phone calls (since our break-up) from my ex to inform me of her latest suicide attempt, and then the remorse and tears over the ending of our relationship. And the angry reminders that a "relationship is a two-way street, you know, Donna!" Yes, a relationship is a two-way street. Abuse isn't necessarily. My point is: the abuse doesn't always end with the divorce.

I still don't know why, when it is so common to grow up with violence in all its forms, that some people go on to continue the tradition of violence and some people manage to rise above that particular training and do good work and lead loving lives. I don't know what makes the difference.

I still have not found it in myself to forgive her. I sometimes think that if I forgive her that it will somehow make me vulnerable to her again. I'll never trust her to put my rights ahead of her violent impulses.

Early on, when Blair and I were first putting out literature on the RUTH support group, we were asked, "So? Who's battering the lesbians?" *Cringe.* Some dykes tried to explain my own experience away by pointing out all the "stress factors" in my relationship. There was an age difference. We were of different racial and class backgrounds. She was more educated than I...perhaps we were unconsciously acting out "roles."

These arguments imply a belief that somewhere there is an understandable reason for battering. Enough stress, enough complicating factors, enough "provocation" and violence is bound to occur. No! We've learned better than that after all these years providing safe space for straight women.

There are powerful forces here at work against the battered lesbian. They are called Shame and Denial. Not only does the battered lesbian or gay man feel the same doubt and guilt associated with victimization, there is also the additional pressure caused by a community which has, up until recently, buried its collective head in the sand. When pushed to confront the problem of women abusing women, the discomfort and anger experienced by the community has, at times, been leveled against the victim.

If a straight woman shows up with black eyes, swollen lips, and broken arms and a story about walking into doors, falling down stairs, *whatever,* any one of us would assume violence to be the true culprit. But when the same thing happens to our sister, we often don't see it. I was as guilty of this form of denial as anyone.

A word about the shelter community:

Lesbians laid much of the groundwork of the feminist theory around why and how violence against women occurs — some of which our own experience forces us to revise, the main point being that we can no longer afford to view violence as exclusively a male-against-female phenomenon, but rather as a control issue. As we began gaining more acceptance and support for the work of providing safe space for batttered women in mainstream society, receiving various forms of public and private funding, we were forced to become more closeted in order to attract and maintain that mainstream community support. Many lesbians turned their positions over to straight workers, moving into closeted work or other women's issues. Then lesbians, experiencing violence in our own relationships, turned to these same safe-spaces that we had helped to create and were turned away. Somehow, in the transition from grassroots lesbian staff to mainstream straight staff, some basic information was lost. And we were forgotten.

In some cases, the shelter workers just did not know what to do with us. How is a battered lesbian or gay man different from a battered straight woman (or straight man)? How does one counsel a person of another lifestyle? Which issues are the same? Which are different? Consequently, lesbians and gay men were without safe space and community resources for dealing with their situations or recovering from them. I know of many instances of lesbians and gays being denied help here in my city. My ex's previous lover, seeking shelter one night, afraid for her life, was turned away, ironically by the same institution that later employed my ex as a relief counselor while she was abusing me.

The stories go on: denial of medical assistance to a lesbian who was knifed by a woman she had left; police officers not bothering to make out a report on an assault case; sexual attacks within our own community; a lesbian psychotherapist who is known to have brutalized ten different women (some to the point of mutilation); a gay activist being threatened and terrorized by a former lover, years after breaking off the relationship.

And so the question remains: What do we do with the batterers in our community? What is our responsibility to our brothers and sisters who may become the next victim? What do we do about those individuals who we know or suspect are batterers or battered? Are there creative, *workable* ways of attending to this problem in our communities?

We're learning not to cover up. And not to make excuses for the violence that occurs and not take responsibility for a batterer's actions. We are beginning to demand accountability from those who commit abusive acts.

It's been quite a few years since I've dealt with this issue on a community level and on a personal level. It all seemed quite behind me. Most of it is. I have recovered, for the most part. But in the last two weeks, I found myself writing in my journal (though I had not set out to) about the one incident at the end of my battering relationship when I finally acted in self-defense, leaving cuts and bruises. An incident about which I experienced an almost suicidal sense of shame and guilt. I hadn't realized that was something I carried like a sin. I had to work that one through, and it's five years later. Also, in the last few weeks, I've learned of two attacks in this area. And I cried when viewing *The Burning Bed,* reliving some of the fear, the helplessness, the loneliness, and the perception that death is the only way out.

I've noticed during the course of this writing an urge in me to give my ex "an out." Allow her an excuse for what happened. Part of me still doesn't believe that this happened. Part of me still fears retribution. But I'm not going to allow her or any abusive person an out. I want them all to be held accountable for their choices and their actions.

Well, the sun is setting and I'm getting chilled. There's only one kite left in the sky, connected to a fishing pole held by a man who is being chased by a squealing little girls in overalls. I hope that their relationship is as loving and playful as it looks.

I'm aware that this writing cannot do justice to the complexity of the dynamics involved in an abusive relationship, the specific way in which the results of abuse pervade, crop up and affect the rest of a person's life. I still look for signs of abuse-yet-to-come in my relating with new lovers and friends. It's always there. The wariness.

All in all, I'd rather be writing love sonnets and stories of passion, courage and healing. And then again, maybe I am. In a way.

Love Is Not Enough

Susan Crall

I am a forty-two year old white lesbian. I was in an abusive relationship with a woman who is forty-one and also white. We are both in recovery programs for alcoholism and co-dependency.

I knew when I met her that she was an alcoholic and had a history of violence, including her previous lesbian relationship. I struggled with the issue of the alcoholism but ignored the matter of abuse. At the time I met her she was not drinking. I reasoned, why should alcoholism be a problem for us when we were so attracted to each other and in love? We convinced ourselves that love would solve these problems, if we just let it.

Two months after we became lovers we were living together. The violence first appeared about that time. Her outbursts of verbal abuse consisted of accusations, blaming, denial, storming about and yelling. Much of the verbal abuse and angry outbursts were fueled by her jealousy of my friends and her resentments about money (I had it, she didn't). Imagination and reality seemed hopelessly mixed for her during these incidents. I wasn't able to see things very clearly. Although I would argue with her and defend myself, I made myself accept her harmful behavior.

For many months I was unable to tell what would trigger this kind of crisis. After awhile, I saw some predictability. Danger signals of impending violence (either verbal, or, eventually, physical) were her sarcasm — which became increasingly vicious — her cockiness, a reduction of topics which were acceptable to talk about, her withdrawal and her habit of reviewing resentments, blaming, jealousy, and, preceding physical violence, verbal abuse. My reactions included fear, loneliness and despair. Before and after a violent incident she made me aware of the reasons for her abuse, namely what I had done or not done. Yet even after I thought I could predict an incident, I felt helpless to avert it.

The other side of her violence was an extreme passivity, negative self-esteem and self-pity. She used these tendencies to convince us both that she was not being controlling through her abuse, and was not responsible for it since she was a victim of those around her. In her opinion, she was only standing up for herself when she was being violent. She believed that she could not control her violence because it was controlled by events outside her. I participated in this lie because I only wanted to see the wonderful times we had together, and because believing this denial of hers gave me a sense of control in a basically unmanageable situation.

From the beginning, she regularly informed me of her "uncontrollable" temper and real strength, enough to break every bone in my body, I was told. Fairly soon into the relationship, I began to feel I was walking around in a mined field, that what I said and did could produce a violent reaction. She threatened early on to hit me, once when we were making love. We talked many times about her abuse, but we always ended on the note of her telling me what to do when she became unmanageable, leaving herself with the option to do as she felt.

A few months after we met, she started drinking again. About four months after that, we had our first incident of physical abuse. She was driving dangerously. I wanted to get out at a stop light, but she held me, saying she would hurt me if I tried to get out. I felt overwhelmed, as though I had been raped. When I expressed my feelings to her that night, she took no responsibility for her part and instead got drunk. The incident was allowed to slide by. A few weeks later, she sobered up and remained sober for the rest of the relationship. There were incidents of physical abuse, about eight or nine over a year's time. The majority of them occurred in the car, usually while driving.

Humiliation was a part of many incidents. She would say degrading things about me, I would defend myself verbally, then she would grab me and force me to agree to what she said. It was next to impossible to get away from her during these scenes. I began to react with abuse and became agitated and intrusive a few times in the early incidents. Then I returned to passivity out of fear. However, the fear seemed only to increase her rage. I also ignored signs of impending violence in the sense that I did not leave her presence before it was too late. Usually I was astounded that she was behaving violently toward me.

As part of my attempt to educate myself on domestic violence, I became involved in a shelter movement conference held in town. This activity only made her angrier and more abusive. But, as she could see that I would no longer ignore the abuse in our relationship, she did decide to go with me to a newly formed group for lesbian couples who had problems with abuse. We seemed to make progress, but the violence recurred a few months later. She became defensive and suspicious of the counselor who led the group. She preferred to see her violence as a part of her sobering-up process (just as she had seen her violence as part of the drinking behavior), instead of as a relationship problem in itself. For her, violence was just something I had to accept about her.

Each incident of abuse was more shattering than the last and I decided that if we could not change the pattern of abuse, I would have to leave her. I was becoming over-sensitized, fearful, untrusting, self-pitying. We were unable to find a safety measure by which to control the abuse. I was developing some very bad feelings about myself for allowing the abuse. I had especially bad feelings about my body and my sexuality, directly linked to the violence. I asked for a separation. I thought this would mean an end to the violence. But it did not. We had another violent incident about a month after we broke up. I fought back against her verbal and physical abuse. It felt very degrading. Yet she approved of my response.

Factors in our relationship which I think were connected

with abuse were reduced social contacts, her strong disapproval and ridicule of anything I did which did not include her or coincide with her values. She also was extremely jealous and possessive. We were both emotionally dependent because of low self-esteem; we had unclear identity boundaries and much denial of what was really happening. She tried to laugh off the abuse, a "little" was no big deal. She made sincere apologies, only to do it again. She came to mistrust our two counselors and the friends we had in common. When I began to re-establish social contacts and activities, she would not join me and instead resumed her abuse. Her jealousy and my guilt response seemed to be the main focus of our life.

I want to say a brief word about our sexual interaction. It frequently deepened our loving bond, yet I feel our sex life was an integral part of this abuse. Sex was held up as a great promise of healing, and so it became an area vulnerable to heavy emotional abuse. She often practiced and simultaneously denied emotional domination in our sexual interaction, just as she attempted control through violence in the rest of our relationship. I generally gave in and played the game. I was very loyal to her, though from the beginning, she accused me of infidelity while at the same time told me I was sexually/emotionally inadequate. She wanted all of my sexual energy to be available for her pleasure, yet often withheld her energy. Even my dancing and masturbation were taboo since they were pleasures which did not include her.

I both hated and bought into this aspect of our relationship. Toward the end of the relationship I did not understand how I could want to be lovingly touched by the hands that hurt me. Perhaps I used our sexual connection to keep my anger and resentment about her abuse hidden from myself.

There is a question which often comes to mind. Why did I stay in this destructive relationship well past the time it became dangerous and unhealthy? The pattern of anger expressed violently in our relationship distorted my sense of reality and encouraged self-destructive behavior. Denial of obvious danger combined with ignorance led me to have split perceptions of what was happening. Part of me knew I shouldn't be involved in this self-degradation, another part pretended it would get better, if only...

After-effects still remain after several months. For the first few months I had anxiety attacks as well as dreams of her accosting me. I also had to deal with anger, resentment and guilt, sexual blocks and negative body image, as well as a sense of victimization.

I am still having a hard time looking at my victim attitudes. The core of these attitudes is a set of feelings which include anger, disgust, deep mistrust, resentment, feeling so crunched down that it's hard to do self-affirming things for myself. It seems that if I feel like a victim, I often get victimized. This is really hard to accept. It is easier to be self-destructive and irresponsible to myself by focusing on the other person's problems, refusing to look at my own anger and sense of helplessness. It feels like getting deeply into debt to myself. These are the times in which I feel extremely needy and yet have an impulse to take care of the one who is "victimizing" me.

Forgiving myself, taking responsibilty for the fact that I chose to be in that relationship, and being good to myself were helpful in healing myself. Also, sharing with other women, including a counselor, was very important. To help change victim attitudes I am learning to set definite limits for myself as to what I want and don't want in a relationship. When I'm feeling that I'm out of the victim cycle these limits are a confirmation of my strength and a key for a real change in attitude.

Taking Martial Arts classes has improved my body image and given me a sense of self-empowerment and well-being. Another thing that has helped a lot has been writing about it, including working on this article.

I am writing this to get the issue of violence among lesbians out of the closet. I feel it is important for the lesbian community to be aware of abuse among us and for us to find ways of changing the problem.

Once Hitting Starts

Lisa

Although it has been a year and a half since I left, a day doesn't go by without me thinking about the relationship and what went wrong. My ability to trust people has been at least temporarily damaged. Something inside of me has decided that relationships are not for me, or that I'm not ready to have a relationship. That is the cost and the hard-won knowledge.

But I feel larger, solid, determined. Never will another person or a relationship be something for me to sacrifice myself for. I look back and can see that there was something good. It didn't start with violence and ugliness. It started with summer nights, two women in their early 20s trying to find a way to see each other. Both lived in households where it wasn't possible to be open about the relationship. Meeting at movies and bars until early in the morning—until finally one left her home. Nights of lovemaking, not enough sleep and feeling fine at work the next day— being relaxed and happy. I had found something that I never even knew existed. I never thought that there would be some one person for me, and I now had found her. I think neither of us doubted that we had found a lifetime relationship. The feeling of rightness was there. That was the way we started; I never thought it would end the way it did.

In loving this woman, I trusted her. I was open to her, I thought she knew I loved her. In not trusting me — being suspicious, expecting and seeing negativity where it was never intended, was the betrayal.

The fighting began with intense arguments which were devastating, like no argument I'd ever been in before. I don't think I'd ever been really open to someone before, and when she was angry it was like being stabbed in the chest. She was the source of that pain; she was also the only source of comfort, understanding and the reaffirmation of love which would come when we made up. All I would know was that we still cared for each other and didn't want to hurt each other. Having lost the connection briefly seemed only to emphasize how important it was to me, how much I needed it, how much I loved her. It was, I felt, the only real love I'd ever experienced. I'd spent much of my life stoic, hostile, emotionally distant, and I needed that closeness like I never realized.

One day we had an argument, and she hit me. We were on my motorcycle, I was driving, and all I could think of was what an insane thing it was — to hit my arm and risk our lives! I could have easily dropped the bike, and traffic was heavy. I remember thinking: You ought to remember this, something very significant has happened.

I think that once hitting starts, a barrier is broken that afterwards is too easily crossed. What was once unthinkable behavior is no longer. Once hitting starts, it's like taking something precious and valuable and smashing it on the ground, and seeing it lying there broken and knowing it can never be repaired.

What do you do when there are twenty to thirty bruises on your arms, legs and shoulders and they can't all be hidden? (You can't always wear long-sleeved shirts.) You're stiff all over, and you're ashamed. What can be said if co-workers ask questions? In my case, actually being clumsy made the excuses more plausible. Last night you were going to leave, but where could you go? You have no car to drive away in, no friends who aren't her friends. Family? What would they think after all the years spent trying to educate them about your lifestyle? How would you explain this?

And who is the monster in the next room who did this? She's just a woman like you who is feeling as upset as you are and is temporarily full of remorse. She is the only friend you have, the only one who seems to care. The idea of leaving seems worse than if you try to stay and make it work and make sure it doesn't happen again. Bruises heal and resentment fades back into the routines of work, shopping, watching re-runs of *All Creatures Great and Small,* and driving her to church on Sunday morning.

All seems normal again, but buried somewhere inside is a memory of what "caused" the fight. This time it was receiving a letter from a childhood friend. You will not admit your fear, even to yourself, but the next time a letter arrives you will read it secretly — and feel a little guilty. It's one more "secret" to be hidden, one more compromise. But you're getting along okay for now.

How I left: I vaguely remember a letter to the editor in *Plexus* from a woman who had been battered. In the classifieds I saw an ad for a support group for women who had been battered by other women. I wrote the phone number on the inside flap of my checkbook where it wouldn't be seen and kept it for weeks. One day I took a long break at work and called from a phone booth. I first told my story to a straight volunteer and I asked her if this sounded like a battering relationship. I didn't know whether my situation was severe enough to warrant the label, as I'd never been seriously injured in any of the fights. (I thought battering meant a 300-pound man and a 110-pound woman.)

I felt like I'd given away a secret, and a little guilty for having told someone about us, but I felt *so* relieved. I felt proud and was able to hold my head up on the way back to the office. A huge weight had been lifted off me. Next I talked to one of the lesbians who was organizing the group. She wanted to know if I could come up to San Francisco and talk with her, and I realized that I couldn't. I wouldn't be allowed!

Usually I had been able to convince myself that I hadn't wanted to do what I didn't have the freedom to do. This realization really hurt my pride, and I resolved to get to San Francisco somehow. On a winter day, December 28, the day of the blackout, I went. I met the woman in a coffee shop. We talked. I listened to my words as though they were someone else's story — that "other" woman sounded so trapped and hopeless, and so scared. I remember thinking, "If I only didn't have to go home."

Just going to San Francisco gave me courage. One part of my life no longer belonged to her. I was able to promise myself that if she got violent again I would leave.

Two months later it happened, and I was almost relieved because it was finally over. I remember her choking me and biting my arm and telling me I was insane because I kept laughing. I was laughing from relief and knowing this wouldn't happen anymore! The next day at work one of her friends called me. She had heard that we had broken up and wanted me to know that they (her and her lover) were there to offer me support. I took a break with her, and when she asked me why we had split up, I showed her my arms. She couldn't believe it, and I was embarrassed and ashamed. I didn't know how to explain to her why I had stayed. However, I was able to stay with them until I was offered the use of a small house. I couldn't believe how supportive and nice everyone was. Within a few weeks I had a new home and was feeling incredibly positive. I was on a natural high for six months. Which brings me back to where I am now. Eventually it hit; going from one relationship to another left me with two break-ups to recover from in less than one year, and another move this time to a place of my own.

I have gone into retreat. For the first time in ten years I have no sexual relationship with a woman, for the first time in nineteen years I have no "best friend."

However, for the first time I'm starting to find out what I'm really like as a person apart from the influence of others — on my own.

Will It Never End?

Cedar Gentlewind

July, 1977.
    I can't believe it. Only when I move, feel the aching and see the scratches and bruises do I know it's real. And when I fall asleep at night it all returns in a nightmare of no escape. Two days ago I was so excited. Dave, an acquaintance, had decided to rent me the little house. Such a sweet house with high ceilings, big windows, and magical white pine trees outside the kitchen.

Driving home to Amy's after my meeting with Dave, I was only slightly aware that she would not be pleased. Mostly I was caught up in my own delight. I can't believe I didn't know.

At 10:00 p.m. it was quiet in south Pagedale. I talked excitedly to Tomi about how we could share the house until it was time for him to head west again for the school year.

The three of us had planned to go out for a snack when Tomi and I returned from Dave's, so I ran into the house to tell Amy the news and collect her to go for the food.

Thank god I left Tomi in the car, and left the engine running. No child should ever see his mother beaten, and Amy might have hurt him, too, if he'd been there. Thank god he wasn't there and didn't have to watch.

I ran upstairs, opened the door to the air-conditioned living room and shut it behind me. Sitting momentarily on the nearby sofa I excitedly told Amy that Dave had rented me the house. In the next breath I reminded her that we were going out for food and to come on.

Her initial expression of surprise quickly faded to icy pale anger and her mouth twisted into a thin crooked line. She stood, and in the blink of my eye was across the room pounding on my shoulders and back with her large calloused fists. I tried to defend myself, tearing her shirt as I tried to push her away from me. Her huge size, which had always given me comfort and a sense of security, was now overwhelming. I was terrified. She laughed at my attempts to defend myself. She told me I couldn't hurt her. She said that for every time I hit her she would hit me twice, and twice as hard. I believed her. She was going to kill me if I didn't submit. I started looking for an escape. She kept hitting. She took my face in her hand and bashed my head into the edge of the door frame. One, two, three — I stopped counting — the bashing continued. A memory of Dad bashing my head against the wall of his bedroom flashed before me. Their hands were so big and my head so small.

She threw me on the floor. Sitting on me, her knees on my chest, she began to choke me. I couldn't move under her weight. Her choke tightened. Looking up into her menacing leer, I remembered the story she had told me about choking her ex-lover to scare her, to teach her a lesson. Looking her straight in the eye, I whispered, "I don't want to die. Just stop this and get off of me."

She stopped. Looking at me with great surprise she slowly got up on one knee and then the other. I scooted from under her and crawled to the other side of the coffee table. Turning as I stood up I looked at her with fury and hatred. I grabbed a paring knife that was on the table for defense. As she stepped towards me, I stabbed the empty air between us warning her not to get any closer. Her mouth twisted again into that thin crooked line. She whispered in a snarl that if I stabbed her she would take the knife from me and slice me to shreds. I believed her. Once again, my anger melted into terror. I put the knife back on the table.

She half smiled. She told me I *had* to calm down, that things would be OK. She said I couldn't leave until I calmed down. I thought, you're nuts, absolutely nuts — I've *got* to get out of here.

I watched for her eye to be momentarily distracted from me. I stood there watching, waiting patiently for what seemed like a long time, controlling my fear and my anger, waiting for my chance.

It came. She looked away for a split second towards the window, I ran in the opposite direction. Over her bed and into my room slamming the door behind me. She was after me in a flash, at the door almost as soon as it slammed shut, pushing on it. I pushed as hard as I could to keep it shut. Suddenly she was gone, running around to the other door to my room. I dashed across the dark room to hold the other door as she tried to push it open. With all my might I pushed. Then she was gone heading back to the other door.

Somewhere in the running and pushing a plan crystallized in my mind. I would hold the door just enough — and I would know when just enough had happened — then I would let go of the door, jump back towards the other door, throw the chair in the path between us and escape out the other door. Hopefully she would not see the chair in the dark.

I held the door just long enough, then let go. The plan worked. As I ran down the hall I could hear her fall on the chair. I could hear her screaming for me to come back, that she had broken her arm, that she couldn't get up. I thought, good. Now I have time to get out of here. I ran down the hall around the corner and down the first three steps. She was still screaming for me to come back and help her. I thought, you're crazy if you think I'm coming to help you. Then the thought rattled through me that she was going to try to kill me for leaving her there. A violent shudder passed through me.

I stopped, turned, and ran back up the steps and into my study around the corner. I grabbed the shoe box from the shelf and ran back down the steps, out the door, down the stoop steps and out to the car. I handed Tomi the shoe box as I jumped into the car. Terror was still in my heart.

Tomi's thirteen-year-old face melted into that of a scared five-year-old as he asked me what had happened. Hardly able to speak, I mumbled something about Amy beating me, and her on the floor upstairs. We had to get out of there and go somewhere where she couldn't ever find us. We had to hide. Any minute she'd be out on the street hunting me with her .44 pistol.

Shaking almost uncontrollably, I drove off down the street, around the corner and into an alley. In and out of alleys I wove my way north trying to think of a refuge. None came to mind. I drove, instead, to Mary and Sue's apartment which was nearby.

I knew I couldn't stay there, it would be the first place Amy would look for me. But they hugged me, gave me a pack of cigarettes and some clothes to wear to work the next evening. I lit up a cigarette as we talked about where I could hide and be safe. After a couple of drags I began loading the .32 pistol that I had taken from the shoe box. Then I realized that Amy did not know where my sister, Sunny, had recently moved. Perfect. I could go there. Amy had no way of knowing where she lived, the apartment was in Candy's name and Amy didn't even know Candy. I called from Mary and Sue's to let Sunny know the score, put the gun in my backpack and left with Tomi. Again, I took alleys and the long way to Sunny's, fearful that Amy was somehow following me.

Once at Sunny's I fell into sobs of relief. She held me tightly. I had escaped. The nightmare was temporarily over. As I told them what had happened, we began to look at the damage — my torn clothes, the bruises, lumps and scratches on every part of my body, the knots on the back of my head, and the finger marks strawberry printed in a ring around my neck. Not a mark on my face, though. Not a mark on my face. That seemed symbolic of something, but the significance continues to evade me.

We made plans for the next few days, drank a few beers, smoked cigarettes and watched the Bijou theater on TV. At about 2:00 a.m., I finally fell asleep. I awoke three or four times with dream replays of the evening, each time waking just as I realized there was no escape from Amy.

Yesterday I went to work and will go again this evening. Candy and Sunny have helped me with clothes and scarves to wear around my neck to hide the finger-printed strawberry marks from my co-workers' curious eyes. My body is so sore, almost every movement hurts. The replays of terror continue to make sleep fitful.

Why me? Didn't I suffer enough beatings as a child? Wasn't it supposed to end when I got big and left home? What is there about me that makes other people want to beat me? I don't understand. I don't know what to do to make it stop. Is life worth living if I can never escape this kind of shit? Is living really worth this?

July, 1985

I carried the .32 on me for about three weeks. During that time I negotiated with Amy through Mary and Sue to gain access to my belongings in her house. Sunny helped me move my things out of Amy's house. I began to set up my life in the sweet little house with the pine trees outside the kitchen.

Within a month and a half of being battered I was again going with Amy. I don't remember exactly what she said that brought me back, but I do know that she said she loved me and wanted me to give her another chance. At the time, that was enough. That was how I had grown up, battered and neglected by those who had proclaimed to have loved me. That was always my father's explanation of his compulsive sado-battery of me and my sister — he loved us and we needed to be taught how to act right. It was my fault he beat me, they said. I was hardheaded, they said. If I would just act right, they said. (They being my father, mother, maternal and paternal grandmothers.)

So I gave her another chance. After all, when someone loves you they always deserve another chance, I thought. We were together through September and part of October. Then I broke it off again. Things had seemed to backslide and I was fearful that her building anger would again be vented on me. I couldn't take the chance that this time I might not escape, I had escaped so narrowly in July. She was angry and indicated it in a thousand ways. I carried the .32 on me at all times until February of the next year, when her constant harassment of me finally slacked off. Amy still kept track of my doings and I of hers, but from afar.

Three years later, after another relationship was ending, I began to see Amy again. This time it lasted about a month and a half or two months. I broke it off again because I could see her resentment and anger building. I couldn't risk that she might unleash them on me. She said she had changed, but she hadn't changed the way she stored up anger and felt deprived when she didn't get what she wanted. I couldn't chance that she was mistaken about being able to control her violence.

I had returned once again because she loved me and could understand some of my pain. Her own pain mirrored mine in many ways. That was what was important. When she held me I felt loved, understood and safe. That was all that really mattered. In those years love was a scarcity and myself hardly lovable — a childhood reality not questioned for many years.

In fact, it has taken me nearly forty years to realize that I am a lovable person, that many people do love me and many more would like to have a chance to love me.

Clearly, in those years I saw abuse as external. External in the sense that I saw it happening to me, a passive and unwilling victim. In my initial attempts to unravel the mystery of why this was happening *to* me, I wrote about the similarities in all my lover-abusers. I wrote that what I needed to do was find lovers who did not have those characteristics.

It wasn't that simple. Not until 1981, when I took a turn inward and began to haltingly look at my interior, did things begin to slowly change.

Besides finding that I am a lovable and loving person, I found that I can take care of myself, that I need to take responsibility for doing that, and that my safety in relationships and in the community depends upon how well I do it. I also found that personal safety is always created, not given.

Finally, I found that as a result of my abusive childhood I had developed the ability to deny my feeling, intuitive self. As a child this ability kept me alive. I was powerless, small and inexperienced. It was critical that I behave according to expectations — that I not resist my father's violence, that I cast my eyes downward in a posture of guilt, and that I accept my elders' view of reality. Instead of feelings, I had taped messages of their views in my mind which I played over and over, obsessively. These thoughts dictated my behavior and kept my feelings buried.

As an adult, I continued to listen to my obsessive tapes, to accept others' views of reality and behave according to their expectations. It had become a reflex. If my lover wanted to yell at and threaten me, I let her. If she wanted to shove me to make a point when she was angry, I let her. My tapes were saying I deserved it anyway, that if I loved her I would put up with it. My reflex response did not let me heed my feelings that yelling, shoving and threats were dangerous or abusive. Blind to the initial abuses of my lovers, I set no limits or boundaries that could have blocked the escalation of the abuse.

My childhood pattern fed into the mounting abuse — it did *not* cause it. This pattern does not make me responsible for Amy's violent and abusive behavior. She must carry the burden of responsibility of her behavior choices herself. Our behavior patterns are opposite sides of the same coin — abuse.

My journey inward has put me in touch with my feelings. It has brought me some peace and a sense of great strength. I have stopped fearing that every relationship will end in battery.

For Better Or Worse

Breeze

Although I spent a total of fourteen years in two lesbian battering relationships (1957-1971), it was not until my work at a rape crisis center that I became aware of the term battered womon, and thus my own self-identification as "one of them."

The Center was run primarily by lesbians at that time, yet I heard little discussion about lesbian battering—a problem I knew was still occurring in large numbers. I wanted to write about this problem, but my fear of it being used against us and further oppressing gays and lesbians stopped me. I discussed it quietly among my closest friends, one of whom informed me about this anthology. It is for her, and my lesbian sisters, that I reveal a past I have spent the last fourteen years trying to forget.

It was 1957. I was nineteen years old and still a virgin. While I had no real physical desire for men, I had an unresolved need for physical intimacy. During my work as a dancer I met Anna*, who was twenty-four years old and in a relationship with a female entertainer. They were the first lesbians I had met. Fascinated by them both, I was initially attracted to Anna's lover.

---

*Not her real name.

During my original visit to their apartment one afternoon, the three of us lay on the floor listening to an album of Sappho's poetry. That was my introduction to the herstory of Lesbos. Shortly after that initiation, Anna's lover left to do a road show, and Anna and I became lovers. It was a lesbian triangle, with Anna unable to choose for an entire year which of us she wanted. Captured by the passionate romance of this budding affair, I waited patiently for Anna to decide.

Throughout our courtship, she was tender and loving. From the onset of our co-habitation, however, physical violence erupted.

The genesis of that earliest fight occurred over a brief affair I had with Anna's lover, which she had cleverly manipulated to get even with Anna. Guileless, I was completely unaware of the vindictive ruse in which I had become ensnarled. Although Anna and I had no monogamous commitment to each other, I was shamed into guilt and humiliation by her calling me "whore," "slut," "cunt," and "tramp." I accepted her labeling of "cheating" and believed her abuse of me was somehow deserved.

The dynamics of our relationship replicated that of a heterosexual marriage, common to lesbian relationships of the 1950s, and still in practice today in some circles. She played "butch" and I played "femme."

In those days, clear delineation of roles was necessary to prevent one from pursuing the wrong partner! Thus it was acceptable behavior for "butches" to act aggressively and exercise dominance in the relationship. Since I was already successfully socialized to be passive and submissive, I fit neatly into that role as easily with Anna as I would have with a man. Questioning this unequal power relationship never occurred to me.

While I was more independent than Anna economically, I relied on her to make important decisions regarding the household and our lives in general. Emotionally, we were symbiotically dependent on one another. Anna demanded freedom to come and go as she pleased while requiring me to ask permission to do anything other than my work.

Following the initial act of violence, Anna continued to

verbally and physically abuse me. This took the form of slapping, kicking, punching, and physical restraint from any escape I would attempt. Other abusive actions included her forcing me to stay awake all night to listen to her verbal attacks with threats of physical abuse if I refused; smashing and destroying special objects that were usually gifts from her (watches, photos, necklaces, clothing); and picking the lock of doors or kicking them in when I would attempt to hide for safety.

While I no longer recall the frequency of abuse in the earliest stages of our relationship, it eventually became a weekly event, followed by remorse, apology, and promises to "never do it again." The making-up periods involved Anna's intense desire and demands for sex, which I found repugnant, but often complied with to keep peace.

Physically, Anna was much larger and stronger than I. Her anger was transformed into bulging eyes, reddened skin, and increased bodily strength. My defensive tactics were typically "feminine" — scratching with long fingernails and hair-pulling. I also became adept at verbal abuse, learning to do with words that which I was powerless to do physically. Generally, that just enraged her all the more.

Even though my life with Anna had become a nightmare, I remained. Over the eight years of our relationship, I did leave for brief periods, only to return. At one point, I went to live with a relative and began seeing a womon who befriended me. During that time, Anna continued to harass me at work, at home, at my parents' home, and at my new lover's office, often with threats of either killing herself or me if I didn't return to her.

After nine months of continued harassment, and disillusionment in my affair with the other womon, I succumbed to Anna's wishes. She had promised to seek professional help for herself if I would return, which aroused my sympathy and fed into the romantic idea that marriage is forever — for better or worse. For me, the factors that I attribute to why I remained so long in not one, but two, battering relationships are intricately connected to why I chose those partners in the first place.

Without delving into a psychoanalytic overview of my childhood, suffice it to say that I had a negative self-image, deep-seated insecurities, and an excessively dependent personality. I successfully internalized the role of the helpless female who fears being alone and without a mate. Other than working for a living, I had no concept of self-reliance. I passively waited to be chosen by my mates, rather than assertively selecting whom I wanted for a partner. Leaving someone meant that I would have to actually seek other womyn on my own, a thought that terrified me. I had never entered gay bars alone and interpreted it as demeaning, equal to that of a heterosexual "pick-up." Unless someone came to rescue me, I felt trapped!

Without consciously self-identifying as a victim, or understanding the dynamics of gay oppression, I perceived myself a social misfit, perhaps crazy, definitely second-rate, and — because I was gay—passively accepted it all. Thus, in order to feel good about myself, I was drawn to other such victims — womyn I could feel sympathy for, who had life a little harder than mine, yet who seemed to possess a sense of personal power and independence that I did not.

Anna had been physically abused by her parents as a child, particularly by her father, a police officer. Catherine*, my second partner, was sexually abused by a female relative during her adolescence, and was in a heterosexual marriage she detested for over ten years. Thus, in both relationships, we could alternate between the two roles of victim and rescuer in a pattern that bound us together.

None of us ever sought professional counseling out of fear that our lifestyle would be revealed and that any therapist would view homosexuality as "the problem." Anna and I had read all the literature we could find, but that only reinforced our secret fear that maybe we really were "abnormal." To live with that self-image every day is perpetually demeaning and a form of psychic mutilation. On a deep subconscious level, I felt I got what I deserved.

I basically accepted my relationship as common to the "gay

---

*Not her real name.

experience." Most other couples I knew in our lesbian clique also had physical fights, so it seemed to be normal. Although I didn't like it, I saw no acceptable alternative. Our social life was limited to gay bars where physical violence was also the norm. While we disliked the bar scene, as working-class lesbians we found no opportunity to meet other lesbians. The bar atmosphere reinforced violence, jealousy, and self-denigration, and our lack of knowledge regarding diversity in lesbian lifestyles kept us isolated and ignorant. Victimization proliferated.

Like most contemporary couples of any sexual persuasion, we had few acquired skills in communicating or in coping with stress and anger. Likewise, our concept of primary relationships was based on the heterosexual model of jealousy and possessiveness as proof of love, unquestioned expectations of monogamy, and the double standard of infidelity — forgivable for the "butch," unforgivable for the "femme."

There was also internalized pressure for us to stay together forever, even though we knew no lesbian couples whose relationships lasted more than ten years. The average was three to five years. Today I know of many couples together for over twenty years. That factor, itself, played a large part in why I remained with Anna for eight years. It was as though the duration of our relationship was more important than the quality, a phenomenon I believe still exists today for womyn in general, crossing all sexual orientations.

What were the motivating factors that prompted me to leave each of my abusive relationships, and what finally led to success in breaking the cycle entirely?

Throughout our years together, Anna had numerous flirtations and friendships with other womyn. While she denied having any affairs, I was insanely jealous of the other womyn. In hindsight, I believe it was more a case of envy and fear of acting on my own undisclosed attractions. When Anna finally became openly involved with another woman and declared her intentions of living with her, I then became involved with Catherine. Catherine and her partner were our closest friends, which brought an end to both relationships.

There were several common threads woven between Anna

and Catherine. They were former friends and lovers themselves. They both abused alcohol and were biweekly clients of a local physician administering amphetamines (diet pills and shots) to a large number of womyn in the community. It is conceivable that their psychological and physiological behavior was exacerbated by the abuse of those substances.

A major difference between them that attracted me to Catherine was her pursuit of higher education. It was she who encouraged me, by then twenty-nine years old, to enroll in the college where she was working on an undergraduate degree. It was at this point that I began what was to become a long process of breaking away from the traditional values and beliefs of my socialization.

The abuse I experienced with Catherine was more psychological than physical, though both were present over the six years. Like Anna, she was attractive and charming, and sex became a powerful narcotic in our relationship. She was a master at manipulation and deception, practiced since childhood and perfected during her marriage. Consequently I was always in a quandary over what was fact and what was fiction. I grew to be extremely suspicious of her words and actions, especially her involvements with other womyn. She would continually accuse me of imagining things, eventually causing me to question my own sanity and intuition, which resulted in even lower self-worth. Perhaps I was, after all, crazy!

While the precipitating event causing me to leave Catherine was one of her affairs, there were other factors that motivated me to break from that relationship. The primary one was recognition that alcohol was becoming a severe problem in my life. There had been a pattern of weekly alcoholic binges in which I experienced total black-outs, remembering nothing. It frightened me.

Another important factor was that I was nearing graduation from the university. With an undergraduate degree as my ticket to finding professional employment, I felt ready to risk living and being alone at the age of thirty-three. Education helped to open my mind to many concepts I had formerly believed were finite, and for the first time I really began to question how I was living my life.

An interesting side-note is that I left Catherine on Easter, which at the time grieved me immensely. I now interpret the subconscious choice of that day as my own Resurrection! With that came other changes — new friends, a different social environment, learning about my personal needs and skills — what I liked and disliked. My self-worth sky-rocketed. I actually found pleasure in living alone and interacting with other womyn as both friends and lovers.

I became especially aware of personality cues that might indicate a potential for violence in other womyn, with the absolute conviction never to repeat that pattern again. I also became terrified whenever voices were raised, and to this day I will immediately leave wherever that situation occurs.

Until I began writing this article, I didn't see the connections between specific relationship problems I continued to have and my own battering experiences. For example, I have defiantly resisted structured monogamy and serious committed relationships, explaining that they are out-moded and are simply patriarchal systems designed to dominate womyn. To some degree, I really do believe that.

I have also experienced, until most recently, great difficulty in feeling deep intimacy for a lover. I would hold back on those feelings while waiting to see if the relationship would really work. In one relationship, I lost all sexual desire and was willing to settle for affection because it was nonviolent.

Additionally, I have continued to have problems with trust, in myself and others. Because I chose two abusive partners and remained with them for so many years, I questioned my ability to choose a good partner. If I can't trust myself, how do I know I can trust anyone else?

Another problem has been the tendency to totally withdraw from conflict and anger. Since violence and angry shouting has been the common method for dealing with conflict, I still tend to withdraw — through silence or complete removal from the situation. One final problem I also associate with abuse is difficulty in making decisions. Since distrusting my decisions based on previous mistakes (i.e., wrong partners),

I constantly question the decisions I do make.

Dependency issues were an important factor in my experience as a battered lesbian. I am inclined to believe that the dependent personality plays a greater role in abusive relationships than sexual orientation.

Nevertheless, the guilt and shame associated with living a lesbian lifestyle — where one's most intimate relationship is either ignored, invalidated, or publicly denounced — may also promote violence where it might not exist otherwise.

Do I believe that these are the only dynamics involved in lesbian battering? No, I don't. I feel that this is merely the rudimentary stage of exploring an extremely complex problem from many perspectives. My discussion is obviously from the view of the "victim" — "femme"-identified — and herstorically rooted in pre-feminist consciousness.

Love As Addiction

Kate Hurley

Notes for an article about a destructive relationship of mine have sat in a folder for more than four years. My hesitation in writing comes partly from a feeling that "battering" was not really an issue in my relationship, although it was occasionally violent. Also, I do not want to feel I am getting even with Mary, a woman thirty years older than I am, by telling the story. Some women get even with ex-lovers by making them nasty characters in their novels. Others use more direct retaliation; for example, the woman in Los Angeles who tipped off the cops to the zoning violations of her ex-partner's feminist business.

Putting another woman in a bad light by telling our story gives me some ethical twitches, but as Beverly Brown, the author of the article "Lesbian Battery," points out, we feminists can be trapped by "the refusal to name any woman more culpable than another." The woman who is battered is placed at a disadvantage by "the elevation of nonjudgemental-ism in the lesbian community."* These insights help me know that I have the right to tell my story. Mary may someday tell hers. Using pseudonyms at least protects our privacy.

Lesbian Inciter, No. 8 [July, 1982], p. 3.

Here is what I was able to write four years ago, in the midst of my anguish:

I could never write about all this life with Mary because its chief trait has been the friction we create, the constant battering away at each other in words, and that is hard to re-create. Goes on for hours. I heard the bells ring the hour all afternoon, thinking how wastefully the time was passing, in anger and regret.

A Dream: I join a support group for people trying to leave their partners, and we end up being a radical group that blows up the Bay Bridge.

She blurted out yesterday that she resents the influence of lesbian/feminism on me because that means she has less influence.

We began to fight at the Chinese restaurant waiting for our take-out food. On the street she was uncontrollably angry. Scared, I told her to go away. She did, in my new plaid shirt....

Why is the memory of intense struggle so faint when I say yes to her? I want to believe she truly loves me. Sometimes I am so vile to her that I feel constantly ashamed of the way I act. Nobody else calls forth such ugliness from me.

At times when we are together but I am slipping away from her in my thoughts, she reaches out to touch me as if to bring me back into her orbit. This need to dominate frightens me. By an enormous exertion of the will I can move away from her side and then snap! Violently I am pulled back once more. But I have let myself be this way, be the other half of this act.

Last night, furious at her, I hurled my slipper at her and hit her in the eye. Appalled by my violence. I'm as bad as her mother, who beat her with branches and then kissed the welts. Three times today I told her I'd leave her; each time she changed my mind. A desperate situation. I don't think I have the courage to break free.

I feel great tenderness for Mary because she has poured out all her love on me and is so gentle and restrained when I am trying to run away from her. But she can be fierce when I tell her why I think we are not good for each other. "All couples have problems," she says. But I am shocked by my extreme swings —

one day loving her completely with childlike deference and tractability and the next feeling bitterly resentful of her intrusions.

Before the breakdown of this relationship, I could pass as an integrated woman, but I see now I was a walking powder keg of explosive anger, confusions, unresolved problems, and feelings of deep inadequacies. Mary did not cause this mess; she just peeled away the surface calm. But can the woman who rips me open to expose these frightening weaknesses be also the woman who helps me grow to new strengths?

A few months after writing the last entry, I spent a holiday weekend with Mary in the suburban house she shared with a woman her age who was out of town. We clashed violently. The only way I could escape her control or protect myself was to lock myself in the other woman's bedroom. This went on for hours. It was a nightmare. The pattern was repeated other weekends, less dramatically. Finally, after about ten months of being Mary's lover, I decided to go far away for two months; I could think of no other way to break free. Several times earlier I had run away to the country for several days to make a clear break, but she had always been sweetly repentant when I returned, and I always agreed to try again.

Several days after the final break (which occurred on Christmas Eve) I wrote:

Feel relief at being free of the incessant pounding of her personality on mine, the constant pressure, the fighting. It got nasty towards the end. Screamed that I despised her, all her rigid ways. On the last day she used force against me, would not let me leave the bedroom until I agreed to do what she wanted. I was exhausted from several days of strife with her, but I struggled furiously against her (in words). Later, she said she did not want to see me again. But she will have her moments of pain and regret and then try to snatch me back, after February. I hope she can't.

She didn't but only because the long period away, recuperating in the Midwest and letting myself begin to heal in circles of loving friendship, gave me the strength to say no to her, decisively, in the weeks after I returned. Numb and embittered, I could speak to only one friend about what I had just come through, and even to her I could not tell the whole truth. I could not even tell it to myself. Reading these journal entries now makes me uncomfortably aware of the omissions. I was ashamed to admit the extent of our violence, to describe, for example, how she would trap me in my one-room apartment when she was angry at me for not doing something she wanted. She simply wouldn't let me out the door. I would try to drag her away from the door; she would push me back. This pattern would go on for a long time. Sometimes, feeling trapped would make me feel crazily out of control. I cried and screamed, hoping the landlady upstairs wouldn't hear me. Once I managed to pull Mary away from the door, in my fierce anger overpowering the stronger woman, and we scuffled. She fell, with me on top of her. There was a loud crack. Broken rib? I was terrified. I wanted to take her to the hospital right away for an X-ray. She refused, denying she was hurt. Then she astonished me by wanting to make love. I said no, feeling extreme confusion. Fearing that I had damaged her and feeling helpless, I literally fled from town and hid out for several days in the country where I knew she couldn't find me. Later, I learned that she had broken three ribs. Of course by running away I had failed to take care of her when she needed me. I wrote at the time:

Mary needs things to reproach me for. I can never measure up, be good enough. My failures as a lover are her constant theme. Finally, I catch on to this game. Saw my relatives play it destructively, a game for giant egotists. It's called: Please Me But Of Course You Never Can.

This was an important clue to my powerlessness in the relationship but only much later could I connect these words to my need for approval and willingness to be a victim.

In my journal entries, besides passing over in silence our most violent encounters, I was also silent about another painful truth about our relationship. Mary was a stone butch.

In the beginning, I was so naively oblivious to roles that I didn't know I was the femme. A friend had to take me aside and tell me. I dimly realized that Mary affected a butch manner; her money, flashy sportscar and cigar-smoking were signs even I could not mistake, but I simply didn't connect what she was with what her expectations of *me* might have been. With other lovers, the issue of roles had not come up. The first time Mary and I made love, I was bewildered when she wouldn't let me touch her, but I had a personal explanation to offer myself: she was nervous and shy; I was so much younger; she feared I would not be drawn to her aging body. In fact I was intensely sexually attracted. Later I thought: when she finally believes in my love, she'll let me touch her. I would have been incredulous if someone had tried to explain butch/femme to me from the days of the 1940s and 1950s. Even when Mary mentioned that she was something of a misfit in her Greenwich Village life in the 1950s because she refused to buy cigarettes for her lovers, I didn't catch on: You're the *femme*, Kate. She gives. You take. These distinctions were just not part of my thinking.

Perhaps I could have broken free from Mary sooner if our sexual life hadn't been so intense. I say our because she was truly involved and eager, despite the limitations she insisted on. Sometimes we boldly made love in the woods in broad daylight or at the beach, and one night, seized with sexual energy, we made love on her balcony, in a very densely populated neighborhood.

Now I see that love and struggle were fiercely joined. At the time, I had to put the lover experience and the batterer experience in separate boxes. The Kate who loved needed to deny the existence of the Kate who hated fighting and the exhaustion it brought; and the Mary who wanted me back each time I slipped away had to deny that I wounded her deeply.

In those days, I knew nothing about co-alcoholism, although I was certainly angry at the harm done to my family by my drinking parents. Now as I look back on the quicksand year of my involvement with Mary, I see that I was addicted to the violence of our relationship, to the wild swings between happiness and despair, and to my dependency on her. Her approval was like one drink — I always needed more. In those unstable times, I needed my dependency as much as my mother needed her wine and my father needed his martinis. I was conditioned to letting myself get hooked into another person's destructive patterns. But nothing in my earlier relationships with women — self-loving, emotionally whole women — prepared me for the craziness or violence of the pit I fell into with Mary. The more I struggled, the more lost I felt.

The story ends on a rather sinister note, for when my cousin met Mary a few months after our break-up, she was surprised by Mary's strong resemblance to our aunt and to my father; and when I finally saw a picture of Mary's partner of many years, who had died in her early forties, I was struck by her likeness to me.

"The Perfect Couple"

Cory Dziggel

The following autobiographical sketch is offered to battered lesbians and workers in the battered women's movement in order to begin the telling of the story of battered lesbians. I believe this movement will not take lesbian battering seriously until battered lesbians tell their individual stories. It is my hope that workers in the battered women's movement will begin to reach out to the lesbians battered in their homes to offer support and advocacy. As battered lesbians, we also claim the right to live free from violence.

I'm thirty-eight. I think I've been a lesbian since I was fifteen. Actually, I had my first sexual encounter with a woman when I was seventeen. We went to school together. We both had boyfriends. Her name was Louise. We eventually told our boyfriends to get lost because we recognized we liked being with each other more than we liked being with them. After we graduated from high school we ran away together, basically because both of our parents were furious and were trying to get us to stop seeing each other. So we ran away out of state and stayed for awhile. By the time our parents figured out we were serious, we decided we could probably move back into a community near them. We did. That relationship lasted two years. It wasn't violent. We parted friends.

I knew my next lover a year before I started a relationship with her. I knew that she had a bad temper. In fact, on one occasion Louise and I had gone out with Sue and her then lover. I left for a short while on business, but when I returned Louise urged me to leave with her immediately because she had just witnessed Sue assault her lover. We left. I didn't think too much about it even when I subsequently became involved with Sue. In retrospect, I recognized that when I first became involved with Sue, she was pretty violent toward me also, but I concluded at that time that the reason she was being violent with me was that she was breaking up with this other lover and was going through a lot of emotional stress.

Sue and I were living together maybe three days when we were in the bedroom and she became angry and hit me. I immediately left the room and went to another part of the house. Later she came down and apologized and promised that it wouldn't happen again. About six months later we moved to an isolated place. We had been living in the city. That's when things got real bad. She smashed my guitar. She kicked and stomped my dog out the door. She would rip off my clothes. She would pick up pots, plates and anything else that was at hand and throw them at me. She would kick and punch and slap me. I often got black and blue. I could never understand what triggered it. Every little frustration or problem seemed to immediately explode into an exaggerated fit of temper. This happened whether or not the difficulty or frustration was with me. It could be on some professional project she was working on. Sometimes it was on work we were doing together. It never helped for me to apologize. I often tried to say I was sorry in the hopes that I could avert the violence. It didn't work. I tried walking away. That made her even more angry. She would insist that I stay. Sometimes I really couldn't take it and would go to another room. She would follow me and continue her violence. These episodes could go anywhere from one to four hours, depending upon how much energy she had.

The first Christmas we had, I bought her a .22 because she likes to shoot. It was the biggest mistake I ever made. She got mad. She threw the Christmas tree out of the house. I remember it had all blue ornaments. She then took the shotgun and held it to my head. I didn't know if it was loaded or not. I was scared. I don't remember what she said but I know I grabbed the gun and threw it outside with the tree. The gun got scraped. For eleven years every time she looked at the gun she reminded me that I had scraped the gun by throwing it out with the Christmas tree. She never seemed to recall that she had held the gun to my head and threatened my life.

I didn't grow up with this. I didn't know violence. Since apologizing didn't work, since leaving the room didn't work, I started throwing things back at her when she would throw things at me, or when she came to assault me I would just hold her, since I was stronger than she was. This really didn't work either because she would get more and more angry. My fighting back seemed to make her more furious. So I guess what I mostly did was leave the house when she started to get this way because nothing else seemed to work. At first I started to leave with the car. But that was a big mistake because she would stand on the bumper or lay across the windshield, daring me to hurt her. She used to love to mutilate my car. It was one of her favorite things to do in the world. It was the only possession that I really owned and loved; it was my first brand new car. She did lots of things to that car. She dented the hood in with her fist. On one occasion she took it and smashed it into a fire hydrant while trying to run me over. She drove it up over curbs, scraping the underbelly of the car. Sometimes when I would try to leave in the car, she would jump into the car and say, "I'm not getting out, I'm going with you." If I drove away she would then start punching me in the face and chest. She didn't seem to understand or care about the dangers to both of us. She would put her foot on top of my foot and the gas and press as hard as she could. One time I was driving down a country road and she reached over and took the keys out of the ignition and threw the keys into a large field. We spent about an hour to an hour and a half trying to locate the keys. She blamed me for the keys being in the field. One time after she had assaulted me in the car I just got out and told her I was going to walk home. She took the car and left. I walked for a long ways and then began to hitchhike. I got a ride and for some reason arrived at our house only about twenty minutes after her. She saw the absurdity in this and we laughed about it.

What was crazy about all of this was that since I wanted the relationship to work, I wanted it to last more than anything else. I thought that as long as we could fight and then get back together again and work it out laughing at ourselves for the craziness of what had happened, we would come closer together and that somehow the relationship would improve. I recognize this as ridiculous now but it sure felt like that was the thing to do for many years. In fact I did get to know her better, of course, through the years. I did feel closer to her through the years. I did love her more through the years. All of that is true. And somehow I convinced myself that meant the relationship was improving.

All of the above happened in the first year of the relationship. The relationship lasted for eleven years. The violence got worse, just like they say. It became more frequent. Smaller things set it off. I could feel it coming. She began to attack me both verbally and physically in front of other people. The black and blue marks got bigger. The apologies always followed. The promise never to repeat it always followed. After she assaulted me and apologized there was an easier time for awhile. It wasn't great, it was just easier. But the easier times grew shorter and fewer.

You have to understand, I'm a lot stronger than she is, although in the later part of the relationship, when she would get real angry, I wasn't really sure I could stop her anymore. When she would get angry she would get real strong. A couple of times I didn't know if I was going to be able to protect myself.

I remember the time when she choked me and I began passing out, seeing black in front of my eyes. It was then I realized how fragile my life was. I understood that she really could or would or wanted to kill me. Something within me snapped. I regained my strength and got away from her.

I need to say that I was violent back towards her. I didn't start it. But when she got violent with me, sometimes I would get violent back. I hit her car once and put a big dent in it. I once gave her a black eye. But most of the times when I fought back it was to restrain or stop her and not to injure her.

About one year before she left I started drinking. Drinking a lot. We had just moved into a new house. She seemed to be gone or unavailable to me. She told me that she was becoming friends with some women at her place of employment. She assured me that this was all innocuous. I learned shortly thereafter that she had become lovers with one of these women. I was heartbroken. I drank more. One night I got real drunk and I called her at her girlfriend's house and pleaded for her to come home. She promised she would. When she walked into the house I let out the eleven-years worth of pent-up anger at all of the pet abuse, property destruction, and violence towards me. I threw her to the ground. I straddled her, holding her down. I wouldn't let her leave. I remember sitting on her and staring at her. It dawned on me that I wanted to kill her and at that moment I was capable of doing it. I remember how intense my desire to kill her was at that time. But I also remember how that scared the shit out of me. I was real scared of what I wanted to do. I knew I wouldn't let myself do it. I vowed never to put myself in that position again. I let her up and she left.

It's now two years later. It feels nice. Not a dish broken. Not a bruise. No flying objects. The mail box has managed to stand up straight without being run over by an avenging truck. My dog who used to cringe and shake and pee and cower everytime a fight occurred, is now one of the most placid, easy-going, warm animals around. However, it is still true that when friends are around and we begin to raise our voices in hilarity, she becomes agitated and visibly scared.

I can see now that I spent those eleven years of my life tiptoeing around Sue, trying to avoid anything and everything that would make her unhappy. I isolated myself from my family. I also tolerated her racist and classist attacks on my family. I was friendly to the people she wanted me to be friendly to and withdrew from folks she didn't like. All of our friends were our friends. None were really mine. There were two times in the course of the eleven years that I tried to befriend a co-worker. Each time I brought the person home, Sue was obnoxious. She put me down. The situation was too embarrassing to handle. Finally, I just let our friends be the ones she picked. Ironically, the folks who were our friends throughout the relationship were primarily people that I knew prior to the relationship and were my close friends. If she liked them, they became our friends. If she didn't they were not. What is strange now is that even two years after our relationship is over, these folks who were originally my friends are now not friends of either of us. She just destroyed what independent relationships I had with them.

I guess the other reason I'm probably not friends with these folks now is they don't know how to deal with the break-up of of our relationship. They knew us as "the perfect couple." Folks came to us from many states, seeking to find out the magic of our blissful life together! Doesn't this sound crazy? But it's true. So they didn't know how to deal with the break-up. Also, those who became aware of the violence didn't and still don't know what to do with that fact. In some ways, to be my friend is to take sides and that's too scary. They don't know what the consequences would be. Sue is a very strong person. She's very intelligent, bright, witty. She is a recognized professional. She is powerful and has a great deal of charisma. She always seems to be in control of any situation that she encounters. She can be very charming and solicitous when she wants to be. And then there's me. Basically I'm your mellow, laid-back, quiet but loving person. For most people to make a choice between us would take a great deal of courage. I know it may sound strange, but I truly believe they fear her.

It took me a long time to be able to recognize that I was a victim of physical and emotional abuse in this relationsip. How can you be a victim when you give somebody a black eye? How can you be a victim but be stronger than the other person? I think you are a victim if you are the one who always tries to avoid arguments. I think you are the victim if you spend your life tiptoeing around the other person in order to avoid any controversy or frustration. I think you are a victim if you become silent in order to restrain or stop the violence of the other person. I think that you are a victim if you apologize for doing wrong even when you believe sincerely that you haven't done wrong but are apologizing in order to try to pacify and stop an argument. I believe that you are a victim when you begin to agree with someone that their truth is truth even if you know it objectively to be falsehood. I think that you are a victim when you begin to feel like you are going crazy because you clearly understood the other person to say one thing and she adamantly, righteously and indignantly insists that she said something else (though her story may change any number of times within the space of fifteen minutes — each story being incompatible with the prior story) and that you are the one who misunderstood. I think you are a victim when you begin to doubt your own worth. I think that you are a victim when you do things that frighten and scare you just to get away from the other person. I think that you are a victim when you begin to do things that are self-destructive in response to the other person's anger and abuse. I think that you are a victim when you give up on yourself, your dreams, your activities, your pleasures in order to please the other person.

But I know that I am a survivor. I fought back when she would have killed me. I asked her to leave my life when I feared I would have killed her. I·am a survivor because the little kid who first fell in love with Sue — a know-nothing, incompetent, self-doubting kid — grew up to be a clear-thinking, self-confident, strong woman. This all happened even though I was living with Sue under the most adverse and violent circumstances. I am a survivor because I fought with all my being to make that relationship into the trusting, long-term, cherished, honored relationship I wanted. I am a survivor because although I know I still love her, I have totally removed her from my life. I recognize that there is nothing good that can happen between us; that to involve her on any level in my life is to surely invite the violence, the turbulence, the anger back. I am a survivor because I love myself, I am calm and usually patient with myself and others, I am caring and peaceful and have almost no need to exert control over others.

I am now in another relationship. There have been no fights, no violence and maybe five arguments. Neither of us is perfect but it is quite clear that when one person is grouchy, the other person will not receive the brunt of that irritation either physically or verbally. In fact, the grouch is usually confined to a separate room where the other person just doesn't have to deal with it. Somehow the pressure to be right or to prove the other person wrong just isn't there. We are two very different people. We both have clear sets of skills and expertise. Mostly they don't overlap. There is no competition for being the most successful professional. Neither us of us feels the need to control the other person. We are at all times respectful. Some of it certainly has been easier because we are both adults, meeting in our middle thirties, having a clear sense of ourselves, limited expectations of each other and an understanding about what a relationship does and does not bring to life. Maturity certainly helped the second relationship. Maturity itself, however, is not the reason for the absence of violence. We are both committed to nonviolence in this relationship. Nonviolence that is verbal, physical, emotional and spiritual.

I can only speculate about what difference it would have made in my life if there had been a community saying that lesbian battering is real violence, not innocuous fighting among intimates. I can only speculate about what difference it would have made to me had I felt less desolately alone and ashamed. Survivors of lesbian violence must now speak out, for ourselves and our sisters.

PART TWO

Battered Women's Shelters And Work With Battered Lesbians

Lydia Walker

This article is being written so I can share some of my own experiences in working with lesbians who are battered by their partners. I've been a worker in a battered women's project for four years, and I've also had eight years of experience as a therapist. I've worked with at least two dozen lesbian women who have reported being physically abused and three lesbian women who were batterers. My observations, then, will be based on both reports from battered lesbians and from some direct work with lesbian batterers.

Part of my work at the Project involves working with women whose male partners are using the Project's rehabilitation services. Basically, the two people are initially seen individually for six to twelve months, and then, based on the man's progress toward nonviolence and the woman's interest, they are seen in couples work by both workers who saw them individually. Because of the initial increase in danger when a batterer starts rehabilitation services, the couple is advised to live separately; if violence reoccurs while the couple is living together, services will not continue until the woman and children have safe living arrangements.

The reasons for not seeing the woman and man together at the beginning of his rehabilitation work include: the man using couples work as a way of blaming the violence in part on her; the man using couples work to monitor what the woman says and control her access to advocacy; the man using couples work as a means of having contact with the woman; the use of couples work as a way of allowing the man to continue seeking the woman's help for his problems; and the couple having different needs to work on that cannot be addressed together (for example, safety and security plans for the woman if the man should become violent again). At the time I first worked with lesbian women where the batterer was asking for rehabilitation services, I had considerable experience in working with heterosexual couples where the man was asking for rehabilitation help.

I was working at the Project when two battered lesbians, independently of each other, asked to be seen with their live-in partners for help in ending the battering. Without a moment's hesitation or consultation with other workers, I immediately agreed to see both couples in couples work and to work with both people individually myself (of course, both batterers wanted to only work with a lesbian). Neither of the batterers completed services, both couples had outbreaks of violence after the couples work began, and both couples ended services without the battered woman continuing in advocacy meetings. One couple ended services immediately after the second meeting, and the other couple ended services when I said I would not continue couples work while the couple lived together.

The different way that I approached battering when the abuser was a man and battering when the abuser was a woman brought about some very hard self-examination and some thought about *what is different* or similar to battering in heterosexual or lesbian couples. On the personal side, I had to look at some of the assumptions I made about lesbian batterers and lesbian couples. While I did not consciously think about these things, I acted *as if* violence in lesbian couples was somehow different than violence in heterosexual couples, as if lesbian batterers were less manipulative and more likely than men to choose to control their violence, as if a lesbian batterer had a legitimate "demand" when insisting on seeing a lesbian advocate (men often make many "must have" demands because of their "unique" and "special" circumstances), and as if my seeing both people individually and in couples work was not a way of the batterer keeping tabs on their partner. I also acted as if somehow lesbian couples would immediately benefit from couples work, although I knew that this was never the case with men and women.

Attending the National Coalition Against Domestic Violence's conference on lesbian battering in 1983 helped me clarify some of the underlying feelings and thoughts that affected my work with battered lesbians, and to also examine violence I had experienced in my relationships with women. For many women at that conference, it was the first time they had looked at lesbian battering or discussed it with other people; women talked about their disillusionment, fear, and sorrow. Very notable was the fact that many women kept talking about lesbian batterers and lesbian battering being different than battering between men and women, and some women even said that "batterer" wasn't the right word. I joined with other lesbian women who had been battered to confront the conference group with the lack of support, danger and fear that was generated by denial and minimization of battering in the lesbian community.

In looking at myself and my initial work with lesbian batterers seeking rehabilitation services, I think that some of my unspoken thoughts about lesbian battering came from a self-protective stance: "not in the women's community," "what happened to me really wasn't violence." Some of my reactions were also right in keeping with the "ideals" of the lesbian community: women's space is different than living with men, lesbian couples have more equal power between partners than heterosexual couples, lesbian couples "do, should" remain friends no matter what problems happened in the relationship. Some of it was just pure sexism: seeing women as more controlled, more gentle, better communicators, less violent, and more trustworthy than men. These are dangerous perceptions for battered lesbians when they come from the women's community, but how much more dangerous when coming from within the battered women's movement, when coming from their local battered women's project advocate.

While it is hard to accept this, the fact is that in my work with battered women, the only difference that I have ever seen in the interpersonal dynamics and perpetration of violence in battering in lesbian couples is that lesbian women report physically fighting back more often than women who are battered by men. This could be a result of many things such as less size differential, less acceptance from the community to not fight back, more permission from the community to talk about fighting back (note that even here I assume that there might be some difference in the lesbian community's response to battering as compared to the heterosexual community's response). Lesbians who are batterers talk about jealousy and controlling behavior as being "love," they want their partner to "help/rescue" them from their own violence and problems, and they often have very unrealistic expectations of what their partner "is supposed to do for them." Lesbian batterers have the classic "honeymoon phase" of remorse and promises that serve to control the battered woman from leaving or seeking help, and they use both violence/threat and pity/help me behavior to try to keep the woman with them.

Workers in the battered women's movement are familiar with the arguments/myths of "mutual battering"; it's the same idea you hear every time you speak in public and someone says: "What about battered men?" or "Don't you think it goes both ways just about as often?"

Some hard and important questions, then, around the idea of "mutual battering" are: why are female batterers more "believable" when they blame their partner, why do workers see self defense as "mutual battering" if the batterer is a woman, and why is it easier to believe that somehow a battered lesbian is part of the "violence problem" than to believe that a heterosexual woman is part of the "violence problem." I challenge workers in the movement to think about how they would respond to a battered woman who says she provokes him or that she is to blame as much as him because she hits him first sometimes. I hope that this will generate thought, discussion, and preparation for helping battered lesbians.

Making Shelters Safe For Lesbians

Linda Geraci

Lesbian battering is an issue which has been largely ignored, both in the lesbian community and by the battered women's movement. As a former volunteer at Womanshelter/ Compañeras, Massachusetts, and a current volunteer at My Sister's Place, Washington, D.C., I think we have a responsibility to make our shelter safe and comfortable for *all* women, and an obligation to make battered lesbians aware of our services.

Before any outreach can be done, however, it is absolutely vital to work to eliminate homophobia and heterosexism in the shelter environment. Staff and volunteer training must include specific attention to issues the battered lesbian must deal with, such as homophobia, and coming out to family and friends in the context of involvement in an abusive relationship. In our society the word "lesbian," spoken usually in a whisper, is often used against a woman in a derogatory way. As long as the word "lesbian" has the power to produce fear in people, lesbians in shelter will not feel totally comfortable. It is one thing to intellectually accept lesbianism; it is another more difficult task to be able to emotionally put aside the label "lesbian" and interact with the battered woman as an abused woman in need of support.

A very pertinent and controversial question revolves around funding. If we come out as a lesbian-sheltering shelter with lesbian staff and volunteers, we run the risk of alienating our funders and losing vital contributions. Should we be open about the issue and perhaps suffer financially, or should we deny the lesbians who are in need of shelter and who work as staff and volunteers and suffer morally and ideologically? This is a question which should be given serious consideration by shelter boards and staff.

I think the most important point to be made is that shelters must be committed to *all* battered women: black, white, yellow, or brown, young or old, gay or straight, Jew or Gentile. While certainly the battered lesbian has special concerns which shelter workers must be sensitive to, in the eyes of the shelter movement the battered lesbian must be seen as battered, first, and a lesbian, second. Her needs for safety, support, and warmth, are the same as the heterosexual battered woman. I am reminded of a statement I once read by a lesbian to a heterosexual friend. She said, "If you want to be my friend, you must do two things. First, forget I am a lesbian. And second, never forget I am a lesbian." I think this would be excellent advice in dealing with battered lesbians in shelter.

Establishing and maintaining a non-heterosexual environment is essential so that lesbians in shelter may feel comfortable coming out to staff, volunteers and other women in shelter, should they choose to do so. If a lesbian does not choose to come out this right must be respected. It is important to keep in mind that in the lesbian community at large, battering between women is a non-issue — it violates the idea of a safe, peaceful world of women. In this society where violence is internalized at a young age, men are not the only ones who are capable of hurting another person physically or emotionally. We must confront and combat this in ourselves. A battered lesbian who seeks shelter is making a very courageous step which could cause her to lose the support of many of her lesbian sisters. She needs to know there is somewhere to turn.

I think all shelter personnel should begin and continue to discuss this issue frankly, and to formulate specific ways in which they will address it. It has been ignored too long and it is no less serious an issue than heterosexual battering. People involved in the shelter movement must confront their homophobia and work to become comfortable with lesbians so that they can respond effectively to lesbians seeking shelter. A dialogue must develop between lesbian organizations and battered women's shelters which would enable both to confront the issue and work together to resolve it.

Support Groups For Battered Lesbians

Nomi Porat

As an increasing number of battered lesbians are seeking assistance from domestic violence agencies, an organized response from the battered women's movement is critical. No single group of battered women has been as rejected from services, disbelieved and labelled "divisive" as battered lesbians. The cost of the homophobia which has surfaced in many domestic violence programs in response to this issue effectively isolates lesbians in violent relationships — consequences too severe for the movement to remain silent.

Only recently has lesbian abuse emerged as a legitimate issue to confront programatically and organizationally. This change is attributable in part to courageous individual lesbian staff in domestic violence programs who put their own jobs on the line to advocate for lesbian services. Primarily, however, the consciousness-raising should be attributed to every battered lesbian who challenged feminist ideology by calling domestic violence hotlines for protection from her batterer — a woman. Although many battered lesbians were discounted, and even more recounted their stories in genderless language in order to avoid disbelief, the silence has been broken and services to lesbians are slowly emerging.

For domestic violence agencies planning to develop services for battered lesbians, the most critical work lies in addressing fear about both lesbians and violence against women, by women. If staff and volunteer hotline workers have not examined their own homophobia or assumptions about lesbian relationships, lesbian services offered by domestic violence agencies could actually obstruct intervention and further endanger battered women. In order for an agency to provide safety and support to lesbians in abusive relationships, several preliminary steps should be taken, including the following:

• Ensure agency-wide backing for lesbian services through adopting a *case statement,* which outlines the need for and scope of lesbian services. The *case statement* functions to provide agency unity if lesbian services are threatened by funders or the community at large. Staff consensus on the need for and commitment to lesbian services alleviates the pressure on individual lesbian staff to defend the program. The case statement should begin by answering the question: "Are the agency's services available to all battered women seeking services, regardless of class, race, ethnic background, age or sexual preference?"

• Address staff, board and volunteers' fears about lesbians and providing services to lesbians through offering "Antihomophobia Trainings."

• Provide nondiscriminatory services by redeveloping counseling methods, intake procedures and forms to eliminate heterosexist language which assumes a woman's intimate partner is male. This includes reassessing referral agencies to determine their sensitivity to lesbian issues; developing contacts for referrals to lesbian and gay agencies; and re-examining traditional options provided to battered women such as police intervention, restraining orders, etc.

• Provide opportunities for battered lesbians to take leadership in developing services which best meet their needs.

Although these preliminary steps could require months of staff work, each precaution undertaken saves a battered lesbian seeking assistance from the arduous task of challenging homophobia in isolation. It is not the role of abused lesbians to educate domestic violence programs about their plight, but rather the responsibility of the movement to establish consistent programs which meet the special needs of *all* women.

Outreach for Lesbian Services

Since the scope of domestic violence agencies has been limited to serving primarily heterosexual battered women, more extensive outreach efforts are necessary to begin a battered lesbian support group. Due to recent recognition of violence in lesbian relationships, publicity and outreach for support groups will be more effective when coinciding with community education about lesbian abuse. Removing the stigma "battered lesbians" within women's communities is critical to breaking the isolation for women to join the group. In addition to outreach methods such as media releases, leaflets or "speak-outs," personal contact with and education to service providers — counseling agencies, lesbian therapists, alcohol/drug agencies — are crucial in reaching lesbians who are seeking support. Creating the context in which to discuss these issues within the lesbian community is as important as preparing the agency for lesbian services. This type of groundwork helps break the silence about lesbian abuse as an isolated problem and gives permission to lesbians to identify, label and challenge abusive behavior in their lives.

Support Group Intake

Although many domestic violence agencies use a drop-in model for support groups, in-person intakes are particularly useful for battered lesbian groups. The intake interview allows the facilitator to determine the needs and scope of the group, introduce the domestic violence agency as responsive to lesbian needs, assist potential participants with developing safety plans, and screen out batterers interested in the group. Unlike the heterosexual women's group in which the battering male partner clearly will not have access to participating in the group, there have been many cases where the partner of the battered lesbian attempted to join the group. It is not unlikely that the partners of battered lesbians will claim to be "emotionally battered" when their lovers withdraw and shut down in response to the physical abuse. An "abuser" might also claim to be battered if her lover fought back. "Fighting back" in self-defense may be much more common in lesbian than in heterosexual relationships as a result of widespread trainings in and acceptance of self-defense practices within feminist/ lesbian communities. Yet it is essential for domestic violence workers not to label acts of self-defense as "mutual battering," a term too often used to minimize violence in lesbian relationships.

Function of Support Groups

The support group for battered women, both lesbian and non-lesbian, is often the first time a woman feels safe to reveal to others and personally validate the extent of abuse and suffering she experiences in her intimate relationship. Due to the lack of traditional resources available for battered lesbians and to the widespread denial in the women's community about the existence of violence perpetrated by and against women, the support group is probably the first and only place lesbians can acknowledge violence in their relationships. Support groups function to break the isolation and silencing experienced by battered lesbians, provide an opportunity for doing safety planing, and serve to support the empowerment of group members.

Facilitator's Role

Regardless of the counseling or therapy mode one chooses to use in facilitating the support group, it must be one that supports battered lesbians' empowerment. It is essential to share with the group both the scope and limitations of your role as facilitator. Clear role definition enables the group members to ask for or expect specific needs to be met and will contribute to a sense of safety and control for the abused lesbian.

Support group leaders are instrumental in facilitating positive models for communicative, supportive and nonjudgemental relationships within the group. In acting as a role model within the group, facilitators must be cautious about their own need for controlling the group process. Since control and intimidation are linked to abuse, maintaining control over feelings, group process or discussion topics will further victimize group members. In letting go of control the facilitator allows group members to freely participate within the group.

Format

The following is an overview of a seven week support group for battered lesbians and a very brief description of issues discussed by the group. The topics outlined were suggested primarily by battered lesbians who were in an ongoing group, and thus should be used only as an example in order to give structure to specific issues. It is important to allow time at the end of each session for the group members to suggest issues they are currently confronting.

Week 1: Introductions

Discuss the sponsoring agency's philosophy and group guidelines. Allow the first session to focus on introductions which include why the women are in the group, current situations, fears about participating in the group, expectations and needs concerning anonymity. Confidentiality is particularly important since lesbian communities are often very small or close-knit. Suggest to women concerned about confidentiality that they can choose another name for their lover when referring to her. Explain to the women that not only must they adhere to the confidentiality guidelines set forth, but you too as facilitator will also respect them. To solidify your confidentiality statements, work out agreements among all women, including yourself, on how to respond to each other when finding yourselves at the same events or public places. Never underestimate the extent of abuser possessiveness and control:

a short acknowledgement from an unknown woman could later erupt in accusations, harassment or violence. Encourage each woman to define her needs and limitations, specifically about anger expressed in the group or directed at her.

Week 2: Self-defense

It is helpful to address self-defense within the first few weeks to alleviate guilt many battered lesbians will experience for "participating" in the violence as a means of self-protection. Women who have fought bac'· will continuously question whether they are "appropriate" for a battered lesbian group. Revealing the extent to which lesbians do fight back in self-defense will facilitate more honest discussions. Discussion of these issues as well as nonviolent approaches to self-defense helps demystify the desire to use violence.

Week 3: Setting Limits and Boundaries

An issue common to women, particularly battered women, is the fear of demanding physical and emotional boundaries. In part, battered lesbians are afraid their lovers will leave or become more violent if any limitations are set in the relationship. Or, if boundaries are set she feels no power in the relationship to reinforce her needs. In lesbian relationships issues of merging and identification with one's lover may be particularly accentuated and often result in the loss of one's own sense of self and needs. Useful exercises in this session include *defining* needs, limits and boundaries, and practicing role plays to communicate these limitations.

Week 4: Class, Ethnicity and Cultural Issues

In discussing these issues, it is important to note that there is no correlation between class, race and violence. However, it is important to acknowledge battered women's experiences of invisibility when racism, classism or anti-semitism play a role in the abuse.

The abuse of privileges derived from class, race and cultural differences within violent relationships exacerbate battered lesbians' sense of powerlessness and denigration.

Because cross-cultural and class relationships are relatively common and accepted among lesbians, it is important for the support group to explore the connections between control, domination and power — major sources of abuse — and classism or racism. The group could begin with a brief "go-around" describing both their own class/ethnic background and their lovers' background, followed by a discussion on topics including: how has class status contributed to the batterer's ability to control the relationship and legitimize the violence; how has one's class and/or ethnic background contributed to a sense of powerlessness in controlling one's own life or believing one can attain their emotional and physical needs; or how have racist and/or classist stererotypes contributed to disbelief of the battering by friends or sources of support.

Week 5: Anger

Use this session to provide a safe place for releasing suppressed anger each woman has never expressed to her lover. This might be the first opportunity for many women in the group to express anger without the consequences of attack. During this session, attempt to redefine anger as an emotion which does not necessitate violence. Since the battering partner will often use anger to retain power and control in the relationship (i.e., through fear), affirm that anger can be an honest form of acknowledging feelings, as opposed to a weapon to immobilize others.

Week 6: Sexuality and Sexual Abuse

Conflict concerning sexual issues and sexual violence are quite common in abusive lesbian relationships. Bruises, both physical and emotional, bar any desire for touch or vulnerability. Sexual abuse, including rape and forced domination by use of threat, destroys the last elements of trust left in the relationship. Encourage the group to share these experiences as a means to receive validation for rejecting physical contact. Since too often lesbianism is defined by others through sexual activity, the rejection of sexual partners can bring on accusations about one's "true" sexual identification. Counteracting these assumptions is critical to our mental and physical health.

Week 7: Closure

In the seventh week, evaluate the extent to which personal and group expectations or goals were met, and reflect on changes which occurred during the seven weeks. Facilitate a discussion which allows the group to decide future goals and/ or the continuation of the group. Discussion could include developing ongoing safety plans for group members as well as developing plans to demand batterer and community accountability and restitution. For many battered lesbians, it will be essential to discuss feelings of exclusion from the lesbian community — a community which may often ostracize her and blame her for openly discussing the abuse. If the group is ending, decide on a process by which each woman can close and establish ongoing relationships with the group members. This allows for practicing clarity in separation and breaking through patterns of drama and crisis to escape confronting closure.

This support group model outlines some of the processes and issues which require attention when working with battered lesbians. The various forms and topics possible in a group for battered lesbians will emerge through the individuals in the group and the techniques of the facilitator. Any effort to provide services to battered lesbians is a major breakthrough for the domestic violence movement and lesbian service agencies. Hopefully, the articles within this anthology will encourage domestic violence agencies to initiate services for battered lesbians and unify the movement to reach out to a silenced and underserved population of battered women.

Lesbian Abuse: The Process Of The Lesbian Abuse Issues Network (LAIN)

Ann Strach and Nan Jervey, with assistance from Susan Jan Hornstein and Nomi Porat

LAIN began as a small group of lesbians bonded together by difficult questions. How prevalent is lesbian abuse among us? Each time we discussed the problem, complexities of the issues challenged us. How can lesbian battering exist given the choices one makes as a lesbian? Don't we create relationships with women because they are affirming, nurturing, and free from the oppressiveness so often experienced in the heterosexual domain?

We were torn by our thoughts of "This can't be," and yet our experiences told us differently. Some of us asking the questions knew from personal experience that lesbians can be battered by our female lovers. We were seeking common answers, so we chose to create a group forum in order to do our exploring together. Within the first few months of meeting as a group, more evidence helped us confirm what we already knew. Calls came in to San Francisco community organizations that said yes, lesbians are abusive to other lesbians.

As we came to know more, we wanted to share this knowledge and educate our community. Our questions turned to: What can we do? How can we make our impact felt? What are to be our priorities? As we sought answers, more and more challenging questions arose.

Confronted by denial and disbelief by lesbians themselves, and the invisibility of lesbian battering to most of the world, it made sense to focus on education as an important function of the group.

We were concerned about educating gay and lesbian service centers to help them incorporate sensitive and responsive domestic violence services to gay and lesbian clients. Concurrently, we were working directly with domestic violence agencies to sensitize them to the presence and needs of battered lesbians.

The education was critical but what would we say and what could we cite as sources of our evidence? Clearly, we needed more information. How do non-battering lesbian relationships differ from battering relationships? How do battering lesbian relationships differ from battering heterosexual relationships? What services do lesbians need?

An initial survey was developed and originally intended to be mailed to lesbian therapists in the Bay Area. In an effort to generate a larger response, we decided to also mail the survey to members of the lesbian caucus of the National Coalition Against Domestic Violence (NCADV). Half of the returned responses came from outside of the Bay Area, from NCADV members.

The results of the survey were minimally informative but helped confirm one of our fears — myths about lesbian abuse were prevalent among the women sampled. The women sampled suggested that only "bar dykes" engage in violence, that feminist lesbians are not involved in battering relationships, that only couples strictly locked into butch/femme roles have a problem with violence. Our personal experiences exposed the falsehood of such myths.

During this initial fact-gathering period, groups for battered lesbians and lesbian batterers started at WOMAN, INC., a domestic violence agency in San Francisco. The immediate realities of the women in the groups gave a strong impetus for LAIN to continue to forge ahead with a more focused and in-depth survey.

We wanted more information. With the urging of a new member who took on a school project with lesbian battering as the focus, a handful of women met at least monthly during the next year to begin shaping a questionnaire intended to unravel the myths and misconceptions about our relationships. The following goals were developed during this time period: determine incidence of lesbian battering, determine need for services, note whether need is being met by currently available domestic violence services, and determine whether there are differences in certain factors between lesbians who have been in abusive relationships and those who have not. The target population included a wide cross-section of the lesbians living in the five Bay Area counties surrounding San Francisco. Distribution began in March 1985.

The following examination of the process of developing the questionnaire is self-revealing, both in the shortcomings as well as in the strengths. Coming full circle through loops of debate and conflict became a familiar process. A clear example of this occurred with the issue of obtaining respondents' socioeconomic background. We wondered how to probe, yet tactfully obtain, private information. It seemed important to ask about financial and class status, both present and past. Perhaps background information was more relevant than current information. Should we ask salary questions? What about perceived class background? No, we decided, that is too private; it is not only invasive but also not so clear-cut. Two or three questions just could not provide the necessary information to relay information about class dynamics, privilege, or status. As the questionnaire went to press, direct questions concerning financial and class background had found their way back in.

As the group has done its work over time, members have come and gone and the group composition has changed. With the changing membership has come an anonymity and a loss of our awareness of personal histories. Without this background knowledge, we lose sight that *we* were the very women that we are talking about. A mindset prevails that takes on an "us-them" flavor. It is much easier to refer to *those* lesbians that are abused and *those* lesbians that abuse rather than to refer to myself and my lover or my own history of abuse.

LAIN had ventured into unknown and undesirable territories that no one else wanted to know existed. Even as we did the work, we ran into internal resistance, our own as individuals and as a group.

At times it was difficult to bring in and maintain enough women to sustain group energy at a level to accomplish the necessary tasks. It was difficult to get women from other lesbian groups to join us. The lesbian/gay community as a whole seemed quite concerned about street violence against its members, but domestic violence within homes and relationships seemed off limits.

The process of developing a questionnaire was painfully slow. True, there were practical limits. There was no budget, no paid staff, or time off for meetings. But a struggle was present at a deeper level. We had become quite task-oriented, with structural considerations affecting this process. That we met once a month for two hours, during the day, on a week day, partly to accommodate a group member who worked evenings, meant that many women were eliminated. Our commitment to feminist process with non-exclusive meetings, consensus decision-making, efforts to consider all the "isms," etc., meant that we had arduous, repetitive discussions which tried our patience. At times, we stopped a discussion of feelings because of time pressure. It was difficult for us to set priorities and limits, especially responding to our own expectations and pressures of doing pioneering work and wanting to do it well.

For every one of us the topic was painfully close to home. Could it be possible that the group mind harbored a fear of what it desired most — *results* — evidence of our inhumanity to ourselves and our sisters? And once we had the results, the evidence, what would we *do* with it? And what about the sure-to-be encountered criticism? Such as: this study isn't reliable; the questions are too scientific, classist, racist, or biased. That would leave us all vulnerable to even more criticism.

By probing into this subject, we risked the possibility that the issue of lesbian abuse might split our community; we risked the same dynamic that heterosexual women have been up against: expose the abuse and be criticized for "breaking up the family." The lesbian community is a loosely knit, fragile family at best and crucial to many women. We were reminded that, as much as we would like to believe that we can create a subculture, separate and defiant of the white male system, particularly its valuing of violence and aggression, we have all been imprinted by patriarchal society. And when we hold tightly to these beliefs, which not all lesbians share, it can become even more difficult for us to talk about violence against other women, of the abuse in our own relationships. The silence can be deafening.

Through the process of developing a questionnaire, scattered discussions and remnants appeared of how these issues affect our daily lives. It was difficult to integrate personal sharing with the completion of tasks and the desire for a product. It was difficult to move back and forth between emotional sharing and the task at hand. The desire for a finished product most often won out. We seemed to fear that if we were too personal we wouldn't get the work done. Either share feelings or produce a product, but not both. What a familiar split. There were many feelings being tapped, obvious from the extent of conflict and yet we never really got to disclosing ourselves. Here we were, creating questions where we were asking women to examine themselves and be vulnerable and yet we had an impossible time doing that ourselves.

Discussion of single issues provided a good indication of how emotionally stressed we felt about each issue. The more challenged and frightened we were feeling, the more objectifying we managed to be. When an issue would strike close to home, we talked about it as if it were "out there." It was painful to find ourselves in this dilemma.

Whenever the tough spots would come, there might be an internal flash of "we've encountered this before. It won't be as difficult this time." No matter how many times it comes around, the emotions are somewhere inside. Our individual emotional responses were colored by how our relationships were progressing at the time *and* how one was feeling about the "lesbian community" at a given moment.

As a group we had much empathy and identification with battered lesbians, yet the group was greatly split in our judgements and support of sadomasochism. The extent of conflict was substantial and excluded the possibility of self-disclosure. No one in the group felt safe, particularly those involved in s/m sex to disclose their sexuality.

Questions that arose that were left unanswered included: Have we developed a concept of healthy sexual relationships and does it include s/m? What does consent mean and what are the limits of consent in this culture? Can s/m be a healthy/ therapeutic form of dealing with power or is s/m sanctioned battering? Are s/m couples at high risk for battering? Is it true that much of what is sexual play has a bad s/m name?

The conflict was so great at times that impatience took over. We were not immune from the pressure to be perfect and the humane desire to do something valuable and worthwhile. Struggles over words and phrases tried our patience with each other.

Just as we wanted to support ourselves emotionally and have a polished questionnaire, we also wanted to begin getting information back from women as quickly as possible. When our process bogged us down, we struggled with the feared consequences. If we don't get this project done, women will continue to suffer on a daily basis. Yet how could we help ourselves if we didn't talk about how the work was affecting our own lives?

The struggle for definition of terms was ongoing. How do we define lover/partner? What do we call women who batter? Am I a batterer if I fight back; how do we differentiate between abuse in relationships and violence in combative situations? We so wanted to instill a sense of power in respondents and we wanted each woman to be able to define her own terms. We had to yield to the reality that to create a questionnaire, we needed specific terms within the questionnaire. This meant making some assumptions and forming our own definitions, limited as they may be. If we did not provide some structure to the questions, we would not get any usable information.

Did lover mean "slept together" or "six month relationship?" We chose not to define lover/partner or put any limits on how someone else might define it. There was difficulty in asking outright, "Have you been abused?" or "Have you been abusive?" Many women, while in an abusive situation may not, at the time, identify it as abusive. We discovered we have many differing ideas about what is and isn't abusive. We chose to let the respondent define this by asking, "Have you ever experienced any of these..." and asked her to indicate what was unacceptable to her about her own behavior as well as that of her lover.

Capturing the essence of an idea in an understandable question was a difficult task. Early in our work, the questionnaire was geared to obtaining responses from women who had been battered. We realized that we might exclude women who had been battered in one relationship and had been a batterer in another. We realized the necessity of creating a questionnaire that was more universally applicable. We wanted to know how many lesbians have been involved in violence in their relationships and in what ways. We asked respondents to focus on one relationship throughout the questionnaire, and additionally, asked if she had been abused or abusive in other relationships.

Slow and frustrating as it was, the group process did result in a broader, more comprehensive questionnaire. Along with the frustration, came satisfaction. The questionnaire is not perfect, but it is good. Many questions have been stimulated by our work, some of which we are hopeful will be answered through the questionnaire. After analyzing the data we will be even better prepared to go further with two of our other goals: education and training. Even though there is much work left to be done, the satisfaction of having come as far as we have is immense.

The initial reponse to the survey has been positive. Women who did not realize they were battered or batterers, after filling out the questionnaire, have sought services. Clearly, it is serving as an educational tool as well as an information gathering mechanism. The distribution of the work continues through the Western Center on Domestic Violence (WCDV) and has resulted in two other questionnaires being developed in other parts of the country. We encourage others who are involved in conducting similar studies to contact the WCDV for information on the questionnaire.

Safe Space For Battered Women

Barbara Hart and the Pennsylvania
Coalition Against Domestic Violence

At the beginning of all community and coalition meetings, as well as in all program literature and conference brochures, there should be a statement that we as a movement take responsibility for providing safe space for battered women at all of our gatherings. We recognize that all persons who have been battered are entitled to be free of fear from assault or discrediting by any batterer in our meetings and literature.

It is our experience that when lesbians who have battered attend community or coalition gatherings, they often act in a manner that disrupts the process or intimidates battered women and advocates. Examples of behavior frequently demonstrated by people who batter in meetings on violence against women include:

• Minimizing and denying their violent behaviors.

• Refusing to take responsibility for their behavior and suggesting that the battered woman's provocation was such as to make their violent behavior understandable, if not justified.

• Persuading the group to identify with the power in themselves and with their potential to batter rather than encouraging the group to consider their own vulnerabilities and their potential to be victims — encouraging identification with those asserting power and control over others.

• Blaming the victim.

• Engaging in power struggles with the women they battered or the group or the facilitators of the gathering.

Lesbians who have battered and have not been accountable to the person battered and to their community of friends should not attend gatherings to work on ending violence against women nor should they be permitted to have a forum in any battered women's movement literature or activity. Even those batterers who have been accountable must recognize that one of the consequences of their violence is that they may have to limit any contact with the person they assaulted/abused. This may mean that the batterer cannot attend public gatherings or movement meetings if it makes the victim of assault feel unsafe — fearful of physical assault or discrediting and unable to speak about her experience and the lessons that she has learned.

The accountable batterer should inquire of the battered woman or her support group about whether her participation in any meeting would diminish/inhibit the battered woman's participation or if she would choose not to attend in order to avoid this disempowering experience.

It is the responsiblity of the community and the movement to assure the safety of battered women (and women who feel vulnerable to assault or humiliation from any batterer). We must ask all unaccountable batterers to leave our gatherings. Even in situations where a batterer has been accountable, the group should intervene on behalf of any battered woman who feels unsafe because of the presence or actions of the accountable batterer. We must also confront accountable batterers about their false beliefs or statements, their verbally abusive behavior, their discrediting, their minimization and denial, etc.

The movement must facilitate caucusing among battered

women in order to assure the sense of community and empowerment that comes from sharing with other battered women.

For battered women's advocates not to accept responsibility for making safe space for battered women is to be complicit with batterers. We must stand firmly with battered women in demanding safe space from violence within our movement.

This lesson has not come easy. Battered lesbians were the first to bring the issue of safe space for all battered women to the forefront of our consciousness. Many meetings within the battered women's movement and within the lesbian community are not safe space for battered lesbians. We appreciate the leadership of battered lesbians and look to struggle with them for expansion and clarification of the concept of "safe space."

Community Organizing: One Community's Approach

Sue Knollenberg, Brenda Douville and Nancy Hammond of The Task Force on Violence in Lesbian Relationships

In Minneapolis/St. Paul, lesbian feminist therapists, lesbians involved in the battered women's movement, and other lesbian activists have become involved in working with the issue of violence in lesbian relationships. Our organizing efforts began in 1980, and a Task Force on Violence in Lesbian Relationships continues to meet monthly. In this paper we would like to share our community organizing efforts, present some of the projects which resulted, and analyze the strengths and weaknesses of our efforts.

In 1980 when the Task Force on Violence in Lesbian Relationships was formed, we were drawn together for a number of reasons. Some of us had been abused in lesbian relationships. Other women who were working as counselors or therapists became involved because of the demand for therapeutic services. Many of us saw the absence of services to lesbians within the battered women's movement as an area needing attention. There was little information available to us at that time about the issue of lesbian violence. A group in Milwaukee, Wisconsin, had written an unpublished article on their organizing efforts which detailed the lack of response to a support group for victims. Lesbians at a battered women's conference in Lake Geneva, Wisconsin, informally spent time discussing the issue. At that time a number of questions surfaced. Did it really happen? Could it be as prevalent as male-female battering? The presence of violence deeply affected our vision of ourselves and our relationships.

The initial focus of our Task Force was to organize a community forum which would provide an opportunity for the first public discussion on the issue in Minneapolis. The resulting presentation included information on the victim and violence perpetrator as well as treatment approaches for the abusive partner. Background and historical information on lesbian relationships was also provided. The response was overwhelming. One hundred and fifty women attended, many of whom openly shared their own experiences with violence. We were surprised and saddened by the magnitude of the problem and the severity of some of the violence. Our eyes were opened by this outpouring of testimony.

In our eagerness to raise the issue we were unprepared for the dramatic response. Women in the audience suggested that we had minimized the violence. Because of the audience feedback we discovered our own ignorance and disbelief had indeed led us to downplay the frequency and severity of violence within our community.

There were few community-wide support services to meet the needs of women wanting to respond to this new information. Shelters were not viewed as particularly supportive, most therapists were untrained, and support groups for battered lesbians and treatment groups for abusers were not in existence. This was perhaps our deepest flaw, opening up this wound and not offering a method for community response.

The Task Force discontinued meeting for about nine months after the community forum. It is difficult to trace the specific reasons for this. In retrospect, our own emotional reactions in response to the intensity and depth of the issue may have surfaced. Attendance at meetings dropped and the energy level steadily declined. We were frustrated and felt overwhelmed by the problem. Conflicts surfaced about a number of issues, including philosophical disagreements regarding the issue of responsibility for the violence; whether the violence was mutual or there was a clear perpetrator of the violence.

In 1982 the Task Force reorganized because of the determination and grit of several members. Rather than focus completely on tasks, we integrated our meetings with more focused discussion about the issue and our personal feelings. We shared our feelings about the presence of violence in our community, philosophical differences between male-female battering and lesbian battering, and the shattering acknowledgement that the lesbian relationships we had idealized were marred by violence. We discussed the issue of sadomasochism at length after a poster was widely distributed in our community by a group titled "Powerplay." We met with representatives of that group and took a public stance against lesbian s/m. A philosophy statement on lesbian battering was developed from our many discussions.

The goals of the Task Force were two-fold: one purpose was to raise the consciousness of service providers (shelters, crisis lines and therapists) and our second primary task was to do outreach to the lesbian community. By 1983, the activities and public nature of the Task Force increased. Our activities included presenting a workshop at the National Coalition Against Sexual Assault Conference, developing a referral list for services, and sponsoring a luncheon for therapists. A treatment group was begun at the Domestic Abuse Project for abusive partners; four women completed the group. We used this information to sponsor a one-day training for therapists and others who were working on the issue. An article in our local lesbian-gay newspaper reported on this workshop. We have continued to receive requests from shelter and other programs for in-service training. A volunteer training sponsored by the Minnesota Coalition for Battered Women, which is presented three times a year for metro area shelters, now includes a presentation on lesbian battering. We also followed up our first community forum with a second in 1984. Fifty to seventy-five women attended. The presentation included myths of lesbian violence, results and information from the abuser treatment group, and an opportunity for community response. What was significantly different this time was that a referral and resource list was available that evening. We spent time in small groups discussing reactions to the material and brainstorming ideas for our community response.

Since then we have developed a number of approaches to providing support services and resources to battered lesbians. Recognizing that existing shelters for battered women were one resource for battered lesbians, Task Force members were involved with providing homophobia training for shelter providers statewide. This training has been followed up by regularly published information on the needs of battered lesbians in the Minnesota Coalition for Battered Women newsletter. Feminist therapists have provided an important resource for battered lesbians, often bridging service gaps until support and self-help groups for battered lesbians could be developed.

Task Force members have used an intervention model developed by the Domestic Abuse Project for use with violent men as a resource for lesbian batterers. This model is designed to eliminate the batterer's controlling and violent behaviors.

The membership of the Task Force fluctuates between seven and fifteen members and is composed primarily of lesbian service providers (shelter workers, state Coalition staff, therapists). This deviates from the grassroots origins of the battered women's movement in which battered women provided much of the leadership and direction. A key goal of the Task Force is to enhance opportunities for battered lesbians to participate and take leadership in our work.

Therapists have been an important asset in the Task Force. This was one available avenue to us as a resource, and lesbian feminist therapists who were knowledgeable about battering became active Task Force members. With this, however, comes the potential to place an increasingly greater emphasis on therapy rather than self-help support or advocacy. It is our hope that individual support and counseling by professional therapists will be supplemented and sometimes replaced by self-help groups and other resources.

The constituency of the Task Force is primarily white, although strong leadership is provided by a woman of color. The absence of more women of color is indicative of the same problems experienced by white feminist organizations and the battered women's movement. It does mean, however, that there are gaps in our outreach efforts and understanding about the needs of lesbians of color.

Homophobia significantly affects the work lesbians and non-lesbians do in working against violence. It was important to us as lesbians to address the issue because we wanted lesbians in the forefront, not reacting to the straight community's inquiries. Homophobia affects us in publicly addressing the issue in a number of ways. We are sometimes afraid of reinforcing the stereotypes that many already hold. To publicly acknowledge violence means that we take a significant risk. Task Force members employed in homophobic settings face very personal risks through acknowledgement of their participation. Many women in the broader battered women's movement are affected by the public acknowledgement of lesbian violence. This acknowledgement forces a deepening of the analysis of sexism and male/female roles as contributors to violence in relationships. To understand violence in lesbian relationships is to challenge and perhaps rework some of these beliefs.

The Task Force on Violence in Lesbian Relationships is continuing to actively meet. Those of us currently involved find ourselves energized by the meetings and challenged by the possibilities of future work. Some of our projects will include facilitating support groups and coordinating these groups with future community forums. We also are exploring ways to formally organize ourselves which would allow us to seek outside funding. We will continue to write about our experience and be a resource for workshops on lesbian violence and homophobia.

Organizing Safe Space For Battered Lesbians: A Community Based Program

*Linda and Avreayl**

We are a grassroots domestic violence safe home program organizing against domestic violence by providing several options to battered women, such as emergency safe housing, food, clothing, crisis phone, support groups, individual and family counseling, transportation, medical, legal, and social services advocacy, children's services, community education, consultation, and training. In 1981 we began offering safety to battered lesbians using the same grassroots safe housing program model we offered to heterosexual battered women.

Background Conditions

Looking back, we think there are several significant conditions that successfully contributed to battered lesbians using our program: 1) several of us are lesbians and some of us are "out"; 2) two of us have been battered in lesbian relationships; 3) many have been in the Domestic Violence

---

*Our workers, by consensus, made the decision that our program's name and most of our advocate's names must remain anonymous. We do not want the many women who have or will use our program or have supported us to be targeted by the increasing anti-woman, anti-lesbian violence because our name appears in their checkbooks, IRS donation accounting or whatever. This anonymity hasn't always been necessary. We used to advertise and be public. Now, we find word of mouth info sharing better serves our safety needs. A sad and angry commentary.

(DV) and/or Sexual Assault (SA) movements since the early and mid-1970s; 4) in lesbian, women's and DV/SA meetings we took a stand against lesbian battering and sexual assault, including sadomasochism, and offered confidential help to those wanting assistance; 5) many of us have worked in several DV/SA programs around the country, and have been activists in our diverse communities, i.e., communities of color, urban and rural, physically challenged, and separatist groups. Through these experiences we were aware that battering and sexual assault between lesbians existed, and that few and poor alternatives to lesbian battering were available. Lesbians were using "straight" DV programs (we know many DV/SA programs have been founded and continue to be staffed by lesbian workers) — either trying to pass, hiding they were lesbians, or identifying as lesbians and then being homophobically targeted and/or refused services.

Philosophical Values

Philosophically, we operate by the following values. Lesbians have a right to nonhomophobic DV/SA services and all DV/SA programs should become nonhomophobic. Responses to violence in lesbian relationships need to come from the lesbian community's awareness and acknowledgement that this violence exists. The lesbian community needs education to be able to identify physical, emotional, and sexual violence within relationships, to understand battering well enough to support victims and their children, to learn ways to respond effectively to the batterers, and to figure out prevention strategies.

Our priority is and has always been to provide safe space for a battered lesbian and her kids to get away from the violence, to help her sort out her options in a supportive environment so she can figure out what she wants to do. We believe this safe space option *must* be available — affordable, within traveling distance, have vacant bed spaces, and really be welcoming to lesbians — prior to regular, ongoing counseling for battering. Phone counseling or brief crisis problem solving are the exceptions.

We emphasize safe space first because so many women have reported increased frequency and severity of violence when their abusers learn of and/or live with the changes from counseling. Increased lethality or the victim's realization that she wants time apart from her abuser mandates no counseling without safe space options for our program.

We have designed our program to be a method of organizing battered lesbians and the lesbian community to work against lesbian battering. We believe the effective response to violence against women and their children is when the programming has social change as a goal, not social service provision.

Rather than expending our resources to conduct needs assessments, surveys or using other clinical and/or social service methods of setting up an institution — and then justifying one's funding with statistical data gathered from surveys or initiating services — we have focused on ways to safely get battered lesbians together to help themselves and on community education and support. Our "least strings attached" funding comes from grassroots fundraising in the lesbian community. We were already providing domestic violence programming for heterosexuals and sometimes lesbians. We did not need any new information to know lesbians are battered; we did need more appropriate alternatives to escape the violence and needed better tools to organize.

What We Did

Initially, we responded to lesbian victims on the chance that when a lesbian came to our program, we somehow knew she was a lesbian, and somehow she figured out which of us were too. After a lot of chance contacts with battered lesbians, we decided to develop specific programming.

We organized community meetings throughout the extended lesbian community in our area, which includes two cities and one good-sized small town; all the rest is very rural.

Where we knew there were lesbian gathering places or supportive "peoples" places, we posted flyers. In scary areas we used phone calls and word of mouth.

At the community meetings, we made a basic educational presentation titled "Violence in Our Lives." We defined physical, emotional, sexual and societal violence. We explained the dynamics of victimization and batterer behavior, how violence escalates, lethality, the effects on our community, the difficulty of breaking the silence, the effects on children, confidentiality, what you can do if you are a victim, a batterer, or know someone who is and what lesbians can do about violence in our communities. We shared current resources, our goals, and then opened up the presentation to lots of questions and discussion.

We posted sign-up sheets for volunteers, including crisis phone, safe homes, transportation, legal skills, etc. and asked for donations of money, meeting locations, childcare supplies and other support. We developed a mailing list right there.

Our first lesbian volunteer recruitment and training resulted in nine committed volunteer advocates. At the same time we trained our previous volunteers on issues of homophobia and violence in lesbian lives. All of us agreed to announce our program wherever we thought safe and to distribute our new cards and brochures. We made lots of lesbian, women's and DV/SA community presentations, contacted referral sources (hotlines, crisis clinics), developed large mailing lists, and recruited more volunteers. These efforts increased our visibility to battered lesbians, and we experienced a consistent increase in calls.

We never gave out our location to the general public, only our phone number and P.O. box. We disclosed specific office and meeting locations on a need-to-know basis.

We offer individual and group counseling. In our battered lesbians group, we use a support group model with problem solving techniques as the basic skills we share. We also share information about DV/SA, that is, what is physical, psychological, and sexual violence; the political/societal context; effects of societal power differentials/oppressions such as racism, homophobia, etc.; the "how to's" of safety planning; the importance of taking one small step each week toward greater safety. We link women with each other for support and encourage them to identify and organize for their own priorities. We help with technical assistance and emotional support.

From our experience we recommend support groups be "drop-in." A woman calls in and we do either a phone or in-person interview to make sure she is the victim (abusers also call), assess for the lethality of the situation, deal with immediate safety issues, outline the services we offer, sign up for childcare, and provide directions to our support group. Childcare needs to be provided free, and the group should be held in a confidential location where confidentiality *within* the group is maintained.

We advertised the group through lesbian community centers, women's bookstores, bars, co-ops, counselors, and domestic violence and sexual assault networks. We sent flyers and made phone calls within approximately a four-hour-driving radius of our area. We then started a travel fund and did fundraising and budgeting to help low income women get to the only lesbian service.

It became clear we had to make money no barrier to receiving services, and to not depend on the group to pay for expenses incurred. We use a zero-based sliding fee scale and no woman is turned away for lack of money. We found it is important to find donated space and materials, and to fundraise for the group costs.

We had been offering anger control (AC) counseling for men who batter, so it seemed reasonable (at the time) to adapt the AC counseling and offer an AC program for lesbians who batter. Focusing on behavior change using cognitive restructuring and behavior modification techniques, we conducted AC groups for lesbians for three and one half years. After much critical evaluation of AC counseling for batterers, we question and doubt if it was the appropriate way to respond to issues of abusive use of power and control in lesbian relationships. We decided that until we had better ways to respond to issues of batterer accountability, more battered lesbian safe spaces, better advocacy within the criminal justice system, and examined other behavior change models more thoroughly, we would stop doing batterer groups. Also, the number of battered lesbians requesting our services increased and we needed to use our resources to increase victim support.

Issues and Questions

We are struggling with several unresolved issues and questions at this point in our work. These need more discussion and problem solving with battered women's advocates and the lesbian community.

Confidentiality

We find it hard to maintain confidentiality for battered lesbians. In the lesbian community, even when a woman leaves the state to be safer, she often finds situations where someone knows someone etc. who knows her or her abuser. We have had to discontinue using some safe homes and change the group location more frequently than in heterosexual battering situations. This seems to happen because lesbian networks are widespread and include detailed storytelling about friends and lovers. We think one solution is to increase the lesbian community's awareness of the lethality of battering and the vital importance of maintaining a battered lesbian's confidentiality for her safety. This is especially important when our community's grapevine is strong and long.

The criminal justice system

When the criminal justice system is often hostile and/or unresponsive to lesbians, legal options available to heterosexual women are often not realistically available to lesbians, i.e., judges not issuing and police not enforcing protection orders for lesbian victims. Lesbians who choose to be invisible and yet want to use criminal justice system options in responding to physical, emotional, or sexual abuse risk not only possible oppressive criminal justice system responses, but also disclosure—threatening their job security, child custody, and personal safety. "Out" lesbians in our area generally are not relying on policy intervention or court remedies.

What is best for the kids?

If the biological mother is the batterer, how do we best help the nonbiological mother when she takes the kids and goes to a safe home? In most cases the biological mother is the one who has legal custody of the kids and batterers have used this against co-parents. This is a different situation than in heterosexual relationships where both usually have legal rights to the kids.

What can the lesbian community do? We know of a couple of lesbians who have become *guardian ad litems* and lesbian households who have been licensed to provide temporary foster care. This helps with kids who do get caught within the system. What about other alternatives?

How can we work to insure the safety of the kids and deal with mandatory reporting laws involving children's protective services, or family courts (when the child's father is involved) who often see any lesbian relationship as an unfit or unhealthy situation for children?

Batterer accountability

Lesbian abusers are learning to gain community sympathy and support. How do we hold them accountable to their victims and the whole community? Batterers will identify as victims. Having been victimized in the past is used as an excuse for current behaviors. Some lesbian counselors, attorneys, and other professionals will sympathize with an abuser with no investigation or specific information about abuse. What about when the batterer does make genuine behavior change? How do we assess for nonabusiveness from a former abuser?

Name-calling

Lesbian battering and the label of abuser is a controversial issue in many lesbian communities. Where there is some stigma attached to being an abuser, some women have used the label untruthfully as a weapon to discredit other women. We have seen power struggles in the lesbian community disintegrate into name-calling and labelling. This confuses the issue of real batterer accountability.

Professionalism

Our program is concerned with the quality of services from some people in the DV, SA, and lesbian communities who believe graduate degrees and models of service provision consistent with mainstream social service funders (for example, United Way or government monies) are more appropriate criteria by which to choose workers and responses to violence. While we know compromise for survival is sometimes a good strategy, the shift dictated by funding sources and professionalism to definitions of what helps victims and who is a properly credentialled helper is distorting basic information we have gathered from thousands of battered women, including battered lesbians, as *they* have reported it to us. The priorities of economically self-serving, status-conscious and homophobic social workers, counselors, attorneys, doctors and other professionals tend not to be the safety of battered lesbians and their children, or stopping the conditions in society that support lesbian battering. Such professionals, are in fact, participating in power differentials that perpetuate violence.

We welcome dialogue, responses and answers to the issues and questions we have raised and look forward to continuing the work to create a nonviolent society where lesbians can have peaceful homes and violence-free relationships.

PART THREE

Letting Out The Secret: Journal Entries, 1982-1984

Sarah

March, 1982

> *when your lover beats you*
> *when your lover beats you*
> *when your lover beats you*
>
> *bruises do not*
> *become metaphors*
>
> *poems don't*
> *heal a thing*

9/5/84

How clearly I remember the way I searched the women's bookstores for some word, some mention of lesbian battering. I would have settled for anything — two lines in *Plexus* or *Gay Community News** would have made a difference. I was desperate for some validation, some proof that I wasn't alone, some scrap that would help explain the feelings I was going through. No, that wasn't it — I didn't need them explained; I needed permission to feel them.

---

*Plexus is a San Francisco Bay area women's paper. *Gay Community News* is a Boston-based gay/lesbian newspaper.

That was only two years ago. After a year of silence, the "evidence" began slowly appearing. A sign in A Woman's Place Bookstore for a support group for victims of lesbian battering. The article in *Coming Up** which I tried to read while driving home from San Francisco, stuck in a rush hour traffic jam on the bridge. The front page article in *Gay Community News*. I happened to flip on KPFA last Saturday, just as the women's show was beginning, and the topic was lesbian battering. I feel relieved that it's starting to be talked about, acknowledged, as if the community is collectively letting out a big secret — a mirror for my own process of beginning to let out my secret. But I also feel resentful: why did I have to go through it alone, why weren't there things around for me?

And now this chance to tell my story. Yet, as I think about writing my "personal narrative," it comes to me in fragments. Bits of the old journal entries occur to me, snatches of memories. It seems that that's the way to approach it. It doesn't feel right to apply a linear form to this content.

9/12/84

I re-read some of the old journals the other night, sat on the edge of the bed at 1:00 a.m. and read them. It's all there. All the contradictory, tortuous stages I went through. I can handle reading about the emotional/psychic pain, but I still cringe as I watch my own denial, my refusal to feel my anger, and my clinging instead to feelings of loss and the urge for a reconciliation. I don't want to accept that that part of me was there — or can't seem to accept it, even though I am trying to accept/love/forgive myself for that time in my life, even though I want to show myself some tenderness. Why forgive? I still talk sometimes like I was the batterer, not the victim. I still blame myself for loving X. after It Happened. Even then I wanted the love to immediately self-destruct, vanish the morning after.

I still feel guilty for putting these words in print.

Coming Up is a San Francisco Bay area gay paper.

Sun. night 10:30 3/15/82
how do I even begin to write about this nightmare
    X. beat me up.
    X. beat me up.
    X. hit me in the face. Choked me.
    Pulled my hair. Twisted my wrists.
    Bruised my arms.

    And verbally abused me for 3 hours, 4 hours.
    Threatened to kick the shit out of me
    if I ever told her to leave my house again.
    If I told anyone. If I came back with
    reinforcements.

She wouldn't let me out of the bed. She wouldn't let me leave. She was a monster. A crazy insane sadistic monster.

The disgust and contempt and hatred in her face as she mimicked me, spit up every intimacy and word spoken in trust. Saying I threw myself on her and abused her that way. Imitating my "oppressive kissing and touching." Showing me how she hated it. Battering me emotionally for my self-hatred! Saying I was a drain and that's why she couldn't stand me. My complaints about my self, my writing, my job. Screaming in my ear. She says she will not leave the house. She will stay there for 3 weeks, she will cut the bed in half, she will kill the cats. She picked up one cat by the neck. I slapped her. She hated me for being afraid of her. She mocked everything about me. Accused me of things I never did.

Everything. She spit up everything. At one point she was about to spit in my face and she laughed when she saw me flinch.

I have to get her out of my house.

It was as if she couldn't hurt me enough. More and more and more. The volcano erupted.

She spoke of her love for me. The love and the hate. How she didn't want to hurt me!

At around 10 a.m. she fell asleep. I waited until I was sure she was sleeping, and then I threw on clothes, grabbed my pack and ran out the door. I had a quick moment of wondering if I should try to take the cats, but I knew I wouldn't have time. I prayed to the goddess to watch over them. I drove as fast as I could to P.'s house, shaking all the way.

I keep looking within me for a source of comfort, trying to remember who it is who can comfort me. Who's missing? Good X. But there is no Good X. This is who she is. Nothing sacred. Everything I've done or said. And yet she said she could say things that could devastate me. To think she was holding back!

A nightmare. I feel traumatized and trapped. I must keep remembering that someday I won't have this pain. God I hurt. And I'm also so numb.

I have to find a way to get her out of my house.

I have never felt so alone.

Why is she doing this to me.
How can I get through this. How.

9/29/84

In retrospect it is easy to see that what happened on that Sunday morning was merely a physical expression of the abuse that had been occurring all along on a verbal level. We had been lovers for nine months before this incident, and throughout that time, there were over thirty episodes of verbal/emotional abuse. I referred to these episodes as X.'s "explosions." Often, they were precipitated by something minor — a misunderstanding or miscommunication between us, a stressful incident in X.'s life. They often came after a period of intense closeness and intimacy between us (which led me, in the beginning of the relationship, to mistakenly assume I was just dealing with a woman who had some intimacy problems.) X. was almost always drunk or stoned during these episodes. And what were they like? Hours and hours of yelling at me, putting me down, accusing me of things I hadn't done, saying she would break up with me, telling me all the things she hated about me, all the things wrong with me. She would yell at me until I cried and then she'd yell at me and make fun of me for crying.

The majority of the explosions occurred in situations where it was difficult for me to escape — in the middle of the night, in hotel rooms, when I was at X.'s house and too drunk or tired to drive home, when she was at my house and would refuse to leave. Sometimes, I stayed by choice, feeling immobilized. On those occasions I would engage in the interaction, attempting to defend myself, or to deny her accusations. What kept me there, I know now, was a refusal to accept the reality of her rage, and an insistence on seeing it through to the other side. A refusal to leave until "Bad X." would go away and "Good X." would reappear.

I found it impossible to reconcile the two incongruent pictures of X. I clung to the image of "Good X." as if "Bad X." were the illusion, as if the batterer were a figment of my imagination. It was easy to hold on to the illusion that she was actually warm, tender and gentle, when in fact each explosion was followed by an apologetic, remorseful, I'll-never-do-it-again X. How dangerous it was for me to make that split. Whether or not she did in fact have two completely different sides to her, she was one person. And that one person was abusing me.

As time went on, X.'s explosions increased in frequency, and they got closer and closer to being physically abusive. She would say things like "I feel like stabbing you in the chest"; she would push me onto a bed; she would look more and more like she was about to hit me. And she did, in fact, try to choke me one night, shortly after we had arrived in California. We were at P.'s house, in a bedroom, and P. and her lover were right in the next room. Yet I didn't cry for help.

What kept me in that bedroom? What kept me from going to my friends right then, right there, that minute? What kept me in that nightmare? What keeps any woman in that nightmare?

10/1/84
Even when things were "good" between us, X. was full of rage. It just wasn't directed at me. She would ventilate about her hatred of white people, but she talked as if I were not part of the group. There was *me* and there was *them*. I was different from them. But during the explosions, I became part of them. She called me white girl, said she hated my white ass, etc. When we'd reconcile, she'd say she didn't mean those things. And back and forth it went. A part of me believed her. But there was another part operating. This was my first interracial relationship. I was coming into consciousness about my own racism, and felt, at the time, that I should listen to everything X. said about whites. That I was, in fact, responsible for the racism she had suffered, and therefore deserved to hear and expose myself to her anger. I'm not sure how much of that was operating throughout the rest of the relationship. I do know that even after she physically abused me, I would not let myself, a white woman, call the cops on my Black lover.

Monday 3/15/82 9:30 p.m.
Write till the pain goes away. Write your broken heart out. I can't bear it, I want to stop feeling, I want to stop existing for a long time and then come back and have it be all over. I want someone to take the pain away. I want to be rocked. I want anything but this. She twists everything, twists it around, saying that I did the wrong thing, that I treated her bad, treated her like shit because I showed up with P., because I asked her to leave the house while I got my things. She said "I know what I did was wrong, but I called you up at work and told you so; I said I would talk to you tonite, I fed your fucking cats. You asked me if I'd be violent and I said no."
She was screaming and crying. She is furious because I don't trust her. The minute she started screaming, P. got me out of there.

I am sick of waiting, of sitting on my rage and my feelings. I am sick of this whole damned thing. 4 hours of her abusing me, brutalizing me, and I wasn't able or "allowed" to defend myself. And now waiting to get into my fucking house.

I won't always feel this pain. I won't always feel this pain. I won't always feel this pain. It's the only comfort. Someday this will be the past. Someday my heart will be closed to her. Someday I will be recovered. Someday I will be healed. Someday I will be loved. Someday I will trust again. Someday this pain will be gone.

I must close my heart to her. Then mend it. I'm going to need a lot of help. I need therapy. I can't imagine ever having a lover again. I can't imagine ever feeling good again.

I feel like a rape victim.

10/9/84

Last night, in spite of my exhaustion, I sat up and read every word of the new *Coming Up* article on battered lesbians, once again feeling regret that no such article had existed for me, once again reading very carefully to make sure, make absolutely sure that I was indeed battered (When will I stop doubting it? Why do I doubt it?).

I was thinking about how no one recognized what I was describing when I used to talk about X.'s "explosions." I think only C. (my former therapist) saw what was happening, long before I consciously did, or before I wanted to see it. She was the one who asked if I felt like X. wanted to hit me. She was the one who said in answer to my remark that "I felt like a battered woman" — "You are." My friends didn't see it, or if they did, they didn't say anything.

What would I have done if they had?

3/17/82

C. called this a.m. and said, "on a scale of 1-10, how are you?" I said 2.

X. calls and apologizes again. She's "very sorry." She's "going to get help." She "doesn't want me to hate her." Then she

gets hostile: "You should be happy now. You have your house
and you don't have to deal with me."
Any tone of voice reminiscent of last Sunday sets my teeth
on edge.
C. said I was allowed to still care about her. P. and J. also
supported that. C. thinks I should change the locks.

10/22/84
I'm feeling really sick from going through the X. journals.
I had to stop, leave my room and come in here to the kitchen
where I can remind myself — you're not in it *anymore*. It's so
nauseating. How could I have stayed with her? How in god's
name did I allow myself to go through all those episodes of
verbal abuse, over and over again, and in between look only at
my illusions of her, believe her apologies, her lies, etc. No, I tell
you what's really sickening is that I saw it, knew it, understood
it — *knew* I was being abused, *knew* how fucked up she was —
and still *chose* to be there. Still wanted her. It's sickening to
think I was that desperate for a relationship.

It scares me to see that desperation in me. Where did it go?
Is it still there? Am I different? Changed? Healed? I didn't
realize how unpleasant writing this would be. I can't even bring
myself to type up the parts where I was feeling starry-eyed over
her, "in love," in between the abuse. It's embarrassing,
shameful, humiliating. I loved someone who told me I was a
piece of shit. Who wants to admit that?

I feel like I want to cleanse myself, run silver light through
myself, go to a sauna and sweat. Get it out.

3/18/82
I feel like I'm falling apart.
Pain everywhere. I seem to have lost my rage — or
misplaced it. After crying the length of Grove St. — back and
forth — I am now stuffing down my feelings with food and
wine. M. asked: Why are you holding it together now? Fear, I
guess. I do feel like I'm gonna go crazy from the pain. Today I

wanted to die.

I keep asking for permission to miss her. Tell me I'm not a masochist.

10/29/84

I can't do this article. I just don't want to go back there, don't want to make that journey into that time, that pain, that ugliness. When I re-read my recent journal entries, I realized that I don't want to keep blaming myself or putting myself down for having been in that situation. I wouldn't allow myself to blame another lesbian battering victim, so why blame myself? I was in it, I got out, I got through it, and here I am, almost three years later, healed enough to talk about it.

Or so I thought. What I'm finding out as I do this is that there's a raw nerve in the center of me and that the further I delve into this past, the closer I get to hitting that nerve. It's raw, it's alive, it still hurts — it's just been buried under scar tissue.

There's a question I keep coming to, a certain point I keep hovering on the edge of, and then I retreat back from it. It goes something like this:

Do all the years of self-hatred, all the years of living in this woman-hating culture make it impossible to ever stop feeling that there must be something wrong with me since this happened to me? Can I ever love myself enough to know and fully believe that I did nothing to deserve such abuse?

3/19/82

Anger and pain. Rage and sadness. How dare she ruin my new life.

"I'll never shit on you. I promise." None of her promises were true.

I still feel on a gut level that she believes I deserved her rage. I will find my misplaced rage and I will separate from her.

11/27/84

What really strikes me as I re-read the old journals from the months following the physical abuse is that I was suffering so badly as a result of it, but I never attributed my depression to that cause. I never even talked about it. I was severely depressed, suffering from sleeping and eating disorders, feeling suicidal and hopeless, and yet all I obsessed about, page after page, notebook after notebook, was how I missed X. and wanted her back. It's astonishing. It's as if it never happened. I mourned for the loss of her as if she had been the ideal woman. When I *was* angry — and there are moments of it — it was because she got involved with someone else, or because she'd say she would call me and wouldn't, etc. Astonishing. And frightening. The same kind of denial that kept me in the relationship all those months continued to operate and kept me wanting the relationship even after she physically abused me.

Oh — I found my answer to the question, "What would I have done if a friend had opened my eyes to the truth of the situation?" *Nothing.* It's right there, in the notebooks — G. called up and gave me a lecture about my hanging on to an abusive lover. It energized me for the day and then I went back to obsessing. My new therapist did try to snap me out of it, but I'd get pissed at her everytime she'd remind me that X. beat me up. What does it all mean? Is it in fact necessary to go through the period of denial — or, rather, is it impossible to avoid it? Or could it be that there needs to be a special kind of therapy designed to deal with the particular trauma, a therapy that could help you get through the denial more quickly? For all I know, there might be people doing that kind of work with battering victims. I just wish I hadn't had to go through so many months of misdirected pain. I wish I had been mourning over myself.

12/28/84

I've just re-read my draft of this article. So what do I feel now that I'm about to type it, send it out to the world? Lots of things. The first is *shame.* I can't get past the feeling. Obsessing about whether or not I should use my real name. Why am I afraid to have people know this about me? Because some part of me still feels ashamed that someone treated me like dirt. Would I feel any different if I had been attacked by a stranger in the street? I don't know. I can't even begin to think about the possibility of my family seeing this. All the years I've spent trying to convince them of the validity and positiveness of my lifestyle... Well, that's really the crux of it for the whole lesbian community, isn't it? Who wants to admit that anything can be wrong with lesbian relationships?

I'm also feeling like these entries only tell a miniscule piece of the story. Ten pages can't do it. I'm afraid that I left out something very important that some woman out there needs to read.

But then there's another voice in me that says: Telling it is enough. Telling any of it is enough. Surviving it is enough. Having grown from it is enough.

I have to keep reminding myself that I've changed and my life has changed. I'm in a positive, nurturing relationship. I treat myself with much more respect and love than I used to. It's an ongoing process. There's more self-hatred to be dealt with. But I *have* learned to love myself enough to know, to believe and to trust that I will never be in a battering relationship again.

Coming Full Circle

Jeanne Cormier

There is something important to write about here: such violence was hidden for so long. When it came out, women, friends, and community turned their backs...or they did not believe, or look fully. In the hope that women will listen to this anthology, I write, wanting us as communities and as individuals to learn to be response-able, responsible where we have not been. I write, too, from having "come out on the other side": where a lot of personal work has led me to feelings of wholeness, of a strong sense of myself, and of some sense of resolution about the abusive relationship. I offer my story as a gift of hope.*

For three years, I was in a relationship with a woman who was self-destructive and eventually violently suicidal. She controlled and manipulated me with her suicide threats and self-abusive violent acts, proclaiming me totally responsible. Had her violence been directed at my body, I probably would have understood sooner that these dynamics were serious symptoms of a battering relationship.

---

*I present *my* experience on these pages. I consciously do not try to explain my lover/abuser's actions, needs, or background.That is for her to do. I am examining myself, my role in the relationship, as well as the community's role.

I met her when I was twenty-two. I was drawn to her deep beauty, compassion, and passion for life. Before a year had passed we made a life commitment to each other, a ritual bonding, a marriage. We dreamed of having a child, a home, a love lasting. The passion of her loving attracted me to her. She was deeply giving of herself to me, though in the end I found that her love was highly conditional.

Looking back over that period, I realize that our relationship was insular — despite the fact that we were both "public figures" in our lesbian community. We were well-known, but we had few close friends in our daily lives. As a lesbian couple, without the social structures and approval available to heterosexual couples, we depended on each other fully for all of our needs — both present and future. She resented my past or long distance connections with family, friends and lovers. I had almost no friends outside of our relationship. Our mutual friends were old friends of hers. She was extremely jealous of all activities that took me away from her (work, visits with friends). She wanted me to love her, only.

Whenever she expressed disapproval of my actions or beliefs, saying they caused her pain, I considered her feelings. She would say, "If you love me, you would do...." Because I did not intend to cause her pain, to hurt her, I slowly adapted my behavior to that which she seemed to need. I *did* love her. Very much. And I tried to make the relationship work by adjusting myself, because I so deeply did not want to cause her more life pain than she had already experienced. I thought that when she felt more secure about my love, that her fears would fade, and she could become more healthy, emotionally.

Slowly, she tried to control my communications with family and friends, and wanted me to sever connections with my past. She told me what to say in phone conversations and letters. She told me my beliefs were weak and woman-hating, and that I should act according to her beliefs. My sexual response started to fade. This hurt her deeply. She developed a fantasy/fear that I truly wanted to return to heterosexuality; that belief became the backdrop for every issue between us. Slowly she began to manifest her fears in self destructive ways. To protect her from abusing herself, I began to avoid discussing sexual issues; my sexual pleasure became unimportant.

From the beginning, I gave up more personal power than was healthy for me. Old patterns of accepting abuse were still hidden inside me and continued in my relationship with this woman I loved. I would speak or think independently; she would become violent towards herself, and blaming towards me; I would adapt. As she became more violently suicidal, I would do virtually anything, taking total responsibility, to stop her. I grabbed knives from her, threw away all razor blades, lied to police and friends, hid car keys, searched the city at night looking for her, ended old friendships, and told her I'd never leave. She told me I should throw her to the ground when she left the house "to kill herself"; and, so I did. Regardless, she slit her wrists and other parts of her body. She overdosed on drugs and alcohol. She put herself in dangerous situations on the street, knowing she was making herself extremely vulnerable to sexual assault. Always, she blamed me and my behavior or beliefs for the resulting pain. Her own fear was so extreme that she could not deal directly with what was going on (that is, that we were in an abusive relationship, and that she had a role in it). I was trapped, scared, and I felt responsible for her well-being.

The emotional strain was finally more than I could bear. I realized that neither I, nor our relationship, could save her. I realized I was being pulled under with her. I knew I had to leave.

The leaving was literally an escape, and a painful deception, taking two weeks to plan and carry out. I arranged for two capable friends to be present when I left, to stay with her, to care for her, to take responsibility for her. I knew I could only leave if I knew she was not alone to kill herself. I arranged a temporary place to stay with friends. I packed my bags, and arranged to have a vehicle that night. I did not tell her I was leaving until that very night, when my safety — the two friends who promised to stay — had arrived. Leaving was the hardest thing I have done in my life.

After I left, with the ensuing exposure of the symptoms of our unhealthy relationship, I left our lesbian community in spirit. At the same time, she remained highly visible. She talked publicly about our situation, and justified her self-abuse, saying that I had caused her to do these things. She admitted herself to the psychiatric ward of a local hospital, for help. When she came home, friends gave her around-the-clock support/supervision/ companionship as she continued her suicide attempts. In this, her friends took over my role of protecting my lover from herself.

Months later — nearly a year — when she sharply realized that I would not return to her, she turned her violence away from herself, and on to me. It was frightening, and ugly. When I saw her in person, she physically and verbally threatened me. She punched my face and hit my body. She shoved me. She harassed me on the phone. One night I returned home from work to find my apartment destroyed; all of my clothes slashed to ribbons, my piano seriously damaged, precious items destroyed or stolen, plants massacred. That night I did not call the police. I did not get her committed into a psychiatric ward. I thought that would not help her, still my biggest concern.

I began to live in constant fear of her surprise attacks, wondering if she would actually succeed in killing me. I have no doubt that if there had been a gun around, she would have killed one of us. The final straw for me happened another evening. As I was standing by a window in my home, an axe smashed through the window, landing before me. I called some of her/our friends, to tell them what she just did. They said they could not help. They would not confront or stop her. One implied that I had asked for it. Her support group had apparently burnt out or given up, so I got no help from them. I felt terribly alone, and felt denied a sense of safety within my own community.

At that point I called the police for the first time. They surveyed the damage, asked questions and encouraged me to file a restraining order. I did so the following day. She was served the restraining order within days. As I had hoped, her violence stopped.

Unfortunately, as other women in battering relationships know, to say "the violence stopped" is something you say after a long time of fearful waiting...wondering if it will start again today or tomorrow, with a phone call or more shattering glass. In the meantime, I found virtually no support within the lesbian community. Of the many many people who supported her those years, I know of only one woman who actually confronted her on her violent behavior against me or herself. In fact it was through the help of friends that she brought me to court, seeking to revoke the restraining order I had obtained against her. Why didn't one of those friends simply tell her that I had every right to a restraining order? Given her violence against me, the order obviously could not be revoked, no matter how justified she felt in her actions. The courtroom exposure of our abusive relationship was a horrendous and humiliating experience. Clearly not knowing what to do with the situation, the judge made an absurd, inappropriate, and insulting ruling to make the restraining order mutual.

Another time, my fragile sense of safety was unexpectedly broken at a holiday potluck with friends. An acquaintance who knew of the abuse — someone I called a friend — lightheartedly and loudly talked to the small gathering about my former lover. She described her voice and how attractive she looked on a recent night. She brought my lover/abuser's body and voice into the room. She spoke of her as one of their community, as one they cared for. It was no coincidence she was talking about my lover/abuser; she was doing so because I was there. I felt stung. I wanted to cry out, "Can't you see how this hurts me? Why do I have to explain? My life has been endangered repeatedly, *intentionally,* by this woman." I cannot even imagine a heterosexual battered woman being subjected to such insensitivity at a social gathering with friends. It felt cruel to have a lesbian woman take away my sense of safety.

At the same time that I felt betrayed by the lack of understanding and resources in the lesbian/feminist community, I was developing a small circle of new friends who provided me with much support. They helped replace and repair my destroyed and damaged clothes and apartment. They helped me obtain health care for problems that had arisen as a response to the extreme stress. They gave their loving embraces and patient ears.

After the violence subsided, I went into an extreme depression. I felt pure hatred for the first time in my life. It was like a knife in my own heart, feeling hatred towards one I had loved so deeply. Pain manifested physically with a number of serious problems, including a painful vaginal growth, edema, hives, back pain, and breathing problems.

Knowing that all of the health problems were directly related to the relationship, as well as to patterns started in my childhood, I chose to initiate a holistic healing process. This approach, dealing with my whole being — emotionally, physically and mentally — took much time and patience. I needed to work deeply, to tend to what felt like the diseased roots of my sicknesses. I moved to a new city, where I felt safe, and where healing could take place. I began to use homeopathy and body work therapy in my healing. I courageously opened my heart to explore and eventually release the pain I had seen, felt, and kept silent for so long.

This growth process took up what I thought I had accomplished at age twenty — when I came out as a radical lesbian feminist. That period marked a sharp "about face" from my good Catholic upbringing and my childhood attributes of passivity, silence and guilt. I immediately confronted my brother for sexually abusing me as a child and felt that my cycle of accepting sexual coercion and manipulation within relationships was over. I determinedly left the evil, dangerous world of men — for Sisterhood. I did not recognize those patterns when they came around again, this time with a woman I loved.

During my intense recovery period, I often asked myself, "Did she psychically take my power from me? Did I need to confront her to get my power back?" I found the answer to be "No." The turning point which brought me to emotional wholeness came the day I was able to face *all* my feelings — even in their seeming contradictions. I could say that I loved her totally, that I was totally afraid of her, that I was uncompromisingly angry at her, and somehow fully compassionate towards her. I could — and can — say that I miss her. I cannot honestly deny or fully transcend any of those feelings; they are deep inside my heart. And there is a great sadness, knowing that I may never be able to see her or talk to her again, this woman I loved so deeply. At the same time, I feel far away from an understanding or forgiveness of the time when I can forgive her for the abuse.

Today, three years after the violence stopped, I feel free and whole. I no longer hold this one painful experience between me and the world, affecting my vision of myself and others. I have truly learned some lessons from this experience. First and foremost, *even love* is not worth certain sacrifices. I can not ever again give up my own beliefs. I will not lie. Second, my body and every woman's body is sacred, to be honored. I will listen to the truth of my body. I can not be sexual unless I desire to be. Third, I can find happiness alone, *and* I can love, free of old abusive patterns.

Recently, I attended a week-end seminar for friends and family of those who have attempted or committed suicide. Sharing stories with people who have experienced the same guilt, horrors, pain, anger and loss was deeply validating. I have learned that taking one's life is one's own decision, that those of us who try to help a suicidal person cannot take the responsibility for their life. Many cities have support groups for the friends/family of those who have attempted or committed suicide.

I wish to give credit to Marcia Macomber, who helped immeasurably in the preparation of this paper.

It Couldn't Happen To Me

Kim

I am a battered lesbian, but I can't forget that I am also a survivor of my family's violence. I believe they are closely linked. I am not afraid to tell people about my experiences and I've come to believe that this is rare. There are some lesbians in my community who are closeted about their abusive relationships — they are isolated and so am I, but I do know I am not alone.

I remember growing up and dreaming about what it would be like to be involved with another woman. I couldn't safely admit it to myself, let alone anyone else. I was in the midst of surviving my family's violence: the incest with my brothers, the physical and psychological abuse from my mother and brothers, and my father and brother's alcoholism. I was my family's scapegoat. I was angry and very hurt by all of them. I remember telling myself that I was going to leave and never come back. I wasn't like these people and I never would be like them. I held onto the dream that someone was out there in the world who would show me that life wasn't meant to be so painful. And someday I could talk about my love for women.

In the two years after leaving home I went through four hospitalizations for my emotional problems and problems I had with drugs and alcohol. I also lived in a halfway house after treatment for my alcoholism — mainly to help further my independence from my family. It was here at the halfway house that I was comfortable talking openly with my therapist about my lesbianism. I was also fortunate to have chosen a sponsor in AA (Alcoholics Anonymous) who was also a lesbian.

I left the halfway house without a job or any financial security. I had been living with friends in a couple of different homes. There was constant fighting in both of the homes I stayed in. I wanted to get my own apartment but I was unable to find a job to support myself. At about this time I was becoming involved in the lesbian community. I also became involved with a woman named Kris whom I had known for a few months through AA. After a couple of weeks, my present living situation with a married couple became progressively worse, so Kris offered to let me move in with her.

I moved in without much thought or money. For the first two months I was totally dependent on Kris. She had control over where, when and how we spent money for the two of us, even after I got a job. We started to have serious problems four months into the relationship when I began school, had my part-time job and started to gain some independence. She had taken care of me, somewhat like a mother. Now I didn't need that or want that anymore. We started to fight, almost daily.

I should mention that Kris had lived through an abusive marriage and she had lost custody of her daughter because of her abuse of the child. In her eyes I was a constant reminder of her ex-husband. Kris was also beginning to treat me like my mother. I felt like Kris wanted me to be totally dependent on her no matter what it took. Whenever I made strides in my financial independence I felt she was threatened by it. And when I made friends and wanted to spend time with them, she would feel left out. My mother acted like this when I was growing up — she never liked any of the friends I had and she kept track of all the money I made when I was working. Neither Kris nor I could forget our past and somehow it had gotten dragged into our relationship.

After my first quarter of college I seriously thought of moving out to get some perspective and my own space. Everything had happened so fast. I hoped it wasn't too late to move out and "start over" with Kris.

When I brought my idea to Kris's attention she would not

listen. She sensed my dissatisfaction and tried everything to keep me with her; she believed if I moved out our relationship would be over. For the next three months I lived with her threats to drink, to commit suicide, to throw me out, and for her to leave me. I remember begging her to stay when she would head for the door in a rage during a fight; I was afraid she *would* drink and I was afraid when she would drive away in her car recklessly. I remember standing in front of the door and getting pushed aside and trying to make her stay. I was always afraid that she wouldn't come back. I remember feeling totally helpless and guilty when she wanted to die. I made promises so she would stop wanting to die. It seemed like I was totally responsible for her happiness. She had told me at one point that she probably loved me more than she loved herself. I also remember the times when she would become furious about her ex-husband — she would throw things and swear vengeance. At the same time she would sometimes comment on how much I was like him. It was not okay for me to leave her but she had every right to throw me out. I felt so guilty for feeling unhappy and for her pain. I felt trapped and very obligated to stay and *be happy.*

I became fearful of her outbursts of anger and I tried so much to please her and avoid any conflict with her. I felt like it was up to me whether our relationship would last. I started to dread going home at night or spending any time alone with Kris. I was an emotional wreck but I tried very hard not to let it show.

At this same time I was dealing with my parents' attitude that my relationship with Kris was just a phase. I was letting so much outside pressure play a big part in my life. I felt if I left Kris I would be showing my family (and myself) that I couldn't handle a relationship with a woman. I was gonna show them— and prove it to myself! I had now lost my perspective totally. I was staying in the relationship with Kris for all the wrong reasons, definitely not for myself. The biggest reason I stayed was because of financial reasons. I really didn't think I had enough money to support myself and I also heard, repeatedly, that I didn't know how to handle money. I was so confused as to what to do, but I continued to try to better the situation.

I started to talk to a few friends about the problems I was having with Kris. A few friends told me to leave and they stopped listening to me until I did just that. A lesbian couple offered to let me stay there if I needed to get away.

After being together for nine months Kris and I had our biggest fight. I came home after school and began to pack my things. I said I needed a few days away — she thought if I left that showed just how much I wanted to work on the relationship. I resigned myself to the fact, after a considerable amount of screaming and hollering, that I should stay. And I bent myself over backwards to show her just how much I cared. Things did not change — it seemed no matter what I did, it wasn't good enough. I felt terribly inadequate as a human being. I felt very frustrated, angry, hurt, alone, and sad.

Three weeks later we had another big fight. Kris became furious and started to throw things around in our apartment. For the first time we fought in front of a friend, a friend who had come over to fix my hair. I tried so hard to remain calm and pretend like everything would be fine — even when Kris started to pack my things. At one point she stormed out and squealed off in her car. When she came back minutes later she was screaming at me to leave. When I tried to calm her down for fear the landlord would hear us, she pushed me up against the wall and told me to stay away from her. She went back into the bedroom and wouldn't let me come in. My friend left abruptly when she was finished and I then called a close friend to come over and help. I went outside to wait for my friend to come.

My friend showed up with her roommate and they took me to a restaurant. I was finally able to cry because I realized I couldn't live there anymore. I knew I had to leave even though I knew that it meant it would put Kris on the verge of drinking or suicide, or she would try to hurt me. We went back to get some of my things and to tell Kris I was going to stay with friends, the lesbian couple. She said if I left I was to never come back. The next day I was encouraged to go to the battered women's shelter.

I was the first lesbian to come to the shelter. And there was a tremendous amount of homophobia. I was pretty much into surviving as I continued with school, my part-time job, work-study, and trying to decide what the hell to do with my life. There were a couple of lesbians working at the shelter who I confided in. It was all so traumatic, the two weeks I spent at the shelter are foggy. I do remember walking to class one day and feeling like I was going to explode into a million pieces and float away. For the first time in my life I had a clear freedom to do as I wished — with no limits. I had never had that before and I didn't know what to do with it. I wanted someone to help me, to tell me what to do because it was too much. I was too scared to make any decision.

I was taking a night class with Kris but because it was the beginning of the quarter I was able to drop it. I took an independent study through the Women's Studies Department instead. I did my paper on lesbian battering, trying to find out what professional services were available for lesbians in battering relationships in the area I lived in. Most of my energy was put into doing the research for this paper, talking for what seemed endless hours with friends, staff at the shelter, and professionals — therapists, lawyers, social welfare services, and persons who offered services on the college campus.

I moved out of Kris's apartment on the day I left the shelter. About a month later our relationship came to a sudden, but not too surprising end. I began to question my existence. After wanting so long to "come out" and express my love for another woman, I had been disillusioned in my first relationship. It was so painful to accept — I was just numb. For a few months I felt a deep sadness and I cried myself to sleep many nights. I was losing friends, my therapist decided not to see me anymore because she didn't understand, my mother was pressuring me to date men again, and I was living in an unsafe place with people I didn't know. I moved in with two friends of mine and concentrated on new friendships, going to work to support myself, and becoming involved with the shelter and learning the politics of violence.

A few of the staff at the shelter and I started a Lesbian Advocacy Planning Committee which met twice a month. And I made plans to organize a workshop to educate professionals and lesbians in our community about lesbian battering. After five months of discussing what we needed to do work on as a group, the Lesbian Advocacy Planning Committee stopped meeting and the plans to organize a workshop were ended. Many of the women in the community believed people weren't ready to hear about this issue. I protested many times to this argument but I was too tired to venture out on my own and follow through with these plans. I am thankful that the battered women's shelter in this area is addresing the needs of battered lesbians. It is going to take a lot longer to address the entire community with the needs of a battering relationship between women.

I have survived another abusive relationship, but this time around I have become empowered by becoming involved. I am not ashamed or burdened with my past. I just think of all the women who live with this secret alone. I am working towards responding to the needs of lesbian women as well as heterosexual women.

Lesbian Abuse: The Story Lies Under Our Wounds

Susan Kresge

I.

I learned to be a survivor. I am only now learning to live.

My father was the warm, affectionate person in my life. He often told me how he loved me, would always back me up. I idolized and adored him, aspired to be as witty, charming, compassionate. But when I most needed him, he wasn't there. When I did tell him what I wanted, he hollered at me, kicked me, beat me up. For years I went to school with bruises on my body, crying.

My mother was just not there for me. When my father beat me, she'd take the other kids and leave.

I learned early that to express my feelings was to get yelled at, hit, abandoned. The only way I knew how to protect myself was to get angry, be defensive or hide. I spent much of my childhood in hiding. I hid mostly in books, in fantasies, in my endless personal journals.

II.

Christmas Eve several years ago. Like something out of an old-fashioned Christmas book, my younger sister and I sat making the traditional stockings while she recounted horror stories of emotional abuse and heavy bouts of drinking by my Dad, during those years when she was the only one of us left at home.

Nearly forty, I was confronted for the first time with my father's alcoholism by the one family member I most loved, treasured, trusted — my sister.

Why hadn't I seen that?
Where had I been all those years?
I had been hiding.

III.
Truth is I never saw her drink.

Didn't have to deal with what I didn't see.

For weeks I went to my job as a mental health executive wearing dark glasses, make-up caked on my eyes and cheeks. Those times when my young secretary asked me about my bruises and black eyes, I made up stories, or pretended not to know what she was talking about.

There were days when, in cold, anxious panic, I thanked the universe that no one on my end of the floor, at work, was in; those days when she would come storming into my office as though driven — loud, hysterical, uncontrollable, hung-over. I was afraid she would blow my cover; did not know what to do.

I felt helpless. Inside I was dead.
I still never saw her drink.

IV.
The train ride from Chicago to the southern part of the state seemed more interminable than usual. Overcrowded, noisy, fraught with a freneticism that grated unwelcome after a day of fending my way around the big city. I was going home, at last,

it seemed. But something in the din of this train lent an ominous note to my homecoming.

The phone conversation with my lover, that afternoon, had been unsettling. She had sounded hurt and disappointed when I told her I was tired and just felt like crashing in Chicago that night; and yet with an insistence that frightened me, she said it didn't matter if I stayed. I felt torn, confused. I really didn't want to move; and yet, I was pulled to go back: drawn by her apparent but unstated desire to see me, and the hurt in her voice.

So I was on my way home. I looked forward to her sunny welcome at the late-night train; to curling up and being held, comforted.

When I arrived she was nowhere in sight. Instead, there to meet me was her young straight woman friend and co-worker, with whom she had spent the evening. A cold panic rushed through me. I had been assured that this woman knew nothing about our relationship, since for her to know could jeopardize my job. What was she doing here? I felt crazy, out of control, betrayed. I barely heard the excuses she gave for my lover, rejected her offers of a ride, ran for protection, feeling guilty for not being kinder and more understanding.

Later — a madwoman — I drove past my lover's house; saw her standing outside with her friend; parked the car, got out. Impatient and feeling foolish, trapped, I called for her to come talk with me. I wanted to run. Did not know why I stood there.

Before I knew what happened, I was on the ground, the hard, wet pavement beating up through my ass and legs. Again and again, she pushed me, beat me, flailing wildly.

Two a.m. and the lights glared brightly throughout the house where I had followed her, dumbstruck, confused. Intimate pictures of us were strewn amidst empty beer bottles across the large living room floor. Panicked, I cried, "You didn't show these to your friends?"

The details blur. She was hollering about how I didn't love her, loved everyone but her; names of women I barely knew were spinning through the air in jealous accusation; and then she was on top of me, jumping and pounding on me, screaming, possessed, pulling, hauling, lunging at me as I tried to duck — still trying to break through with words, still trying to be rational, to understand what was going on, what I had done to prompt this behavior. Pinned up against the wall, my head struck over and over and over — as though something old were keeping me there.

Her boy child's frightened, plaintive voice broke the blows: "Mother, stop it, I love her, don't hurt her..." The nightmare continued 'til dawn, with me persisting in calming and comforting her. I stayed until she fell asleep.

I arrived at my home with enough time to shower and change clothes. Numb, deadened, I remembered that I was interviewing secretaries that day. Driving to work, I was plagued with the recriminating voices in my head, "Never talk to an alcoholic when they're drunk." The words spun 'round: Why hadn't I known that? Why had I tried so hard to make contact with her?

She left me several months later — back in less than two weeks with promises of a life together, special rings ordered at her initiation. I only saw her once after that. The time I drove over 150 miles to the alcohol treatment facility where she was in recovery. She had said something to me on the phone about doing family therapy with her and the boy. When I arrived it was clear that no one even knew who I was; we spent the day with her pushing me away, making excuses, getting sick, returning early.

V.

The pain and shame of abandonment hurt most. The so-called abuse was familiar; it had never occurred to me to leave her for that.

In that relationship I, too, had acted like someone possessed. This drama we were in was not new for either of us. Barely eighteen when she buried her mother (who'd sexually abused her) from alcoholism, her terror and confusion about love were as old as my own. We were locked into a death-dance, compulsively reacting off each other, never really clear where each of us started or stopped. The guilt and confusion over who was abusive, who was at fault — what was really going on — hung like a black cloud.

I never meant to hurt her. But at times when the shifts in her behavior were sudden, extreme, I would reach out and grab her, desperate to understand what was going on... I remember the force of my body as my arm — as though propelled by its own impulses — reached out and grabbed her biceps; my voice distant, foreign, insistent. The times I shook her, flailing, down, more hurt by her screaming not to hurt her than by the months of tyranny.

We are, none of us, unscathed. Alcoholism is a family disease. We have all learned to repress our feelings, to deny pain, to try again and again and again to please the abuser. We are all party to massive denial of addictions, the abuse, the pain. Those of us in co-dependent roles are as addicted to the alcoholic as they are to their drugs. We play out those roles over and over, compulsively seeking constancy, love, the approval we missed at some critical point.

I have chosen for lovers women who have played out the tyrannical roles of my father and the abandoning roles of my mother. I have been the loyal, understanding partner — the victim — and yet, I have embodied in my own behavior my father's helpless rage, my mother's fear and obsessive insistence to know all.

A recent study shows that thirty-eight percent of lesbians are alcoholic; thirty percent are problem drinkers. "For a lesbian, those statistics mean you either are one, or you love one."* These figures do not account for the numbers of closeted lesbians who may be alcoholic or the hidden alcoholics who may be lesbian.

VI.

Clenched in the jaws of his own anger, the old man who once beat me seethed at me during a recent family visit, "You're angry." I reeled internally, years of anguish and guilt splitting like atoms in my psyche: "Yes," I thought, "I'm angry. I'm angry at having been pummeled into silence as a child. I'm angry at living out your lies. I'm angry at pretense, at the games, at still being so careful not to offend, at still trying to please, at not knowing what I want or what I feel. I'm angry at repeating the same painful behaviors over and over. I'm angry at how I've blindly picked partners who have re-enacted the physical and emotional abuse you modeled for me as love. I'm angry at being castigated for my anger."

VII.

She left me because I "was angry."

After the first few magical weeks, something snapped and I never again knew where I stood with her.

A passionate feminist who claimed to have never been angry. Secretive was her middle name. Open and loving one minute, mysterious and impersonal the next. Jekyll and Hyde in the person of this loving woman. For me a familiar lover.

"On My Way to Nowhere: An Analysis of Gay Alcohol Abuse and an Evaluation of Alcoholism Rehabilitation Sources of the Los Angeles Gay Community." L. Fifield (1975) (Contract # 25125. County of Los Angeles.) As quoted in Swallow, Jean, *Out From Under: Sober Dykes and Our Friends* (San Francisco: Spinsters Ink), 1983.

I loved her more, I thought, than I had ever loved anyone. I ran to her again and again, hungry for every morsel of time together, craving those magical times when I felt like the most special woman alive. Like a moth dancing in a flame, trying to save its life, I kept spinning to her different tunes, trying to make sense of the yes/no, come here/go away messages, trying to respond in whatever the right way seemed to be at the moment.

The more confused the messages, the more frightened I became, the more I persisted in understanding what was going on, the more she ran; the more I was blamed for the discord between us, the more I blamed myself, the more I shut down and conceded to salvage my self-respect, she was back enticing me. Each time I succumbed, she turned away. I felt as though I was living out a lie. Her secretiveness increased, as did my silence, my fear to speak. She left the day I found my voice, cleansed by my own self-loving anger.

This time there were no black eyes. I went into isolation for three months, full of pain, shame, terrified of being seen in our women's public, afraid that others would see me as a reject and would themselves reject me. Six weeks into my isolation, I accepted an invitation to a women's event from a trusted friend; the day of the event, I was so anxious that I cancelled out and spent the evening in bed.

I was afraid of running into her. I couldn't handle the rush of mixed-up feelings that I had each time I saw her: feeling like a fool for having been rejected by such a popular woman; feeling ashamed, vulnerable, and not wanting her to see that; feeling excited to see her and afraid to let her see how excited I felt; wanting to appear happy, desirable; wanting her to want to be with me; dreading seeing her with another woman.

Running into her also meant confronting the months of lies and hypocrisy I had bought into, so desperate was I for her to love me. Those lies that I had felt but so studiously denied. The pain of the truth seemed far greater then than the pain of making myself victim to her every whim.

Now I am paralyzed, unable to cope with women, unwilling to get close, be intimate. I do not trust that this won't happen again, that I won't fall for some woman who takes a fancy to me, proclaims her undying love, then turns on me and blames me for her own self-hate, and abandons me; I do not trust that I won't fall back into the trap of playing victim.

VIII.

I look back at that relationship and wonder if she was really abusive; wonder if it's not just me that's messed up. Surely, I believed I was to blame for her behavior. Nothing I did was ever right. If only I had responded sooner, or differently, or more lovingly, things would have been fine and she wouldn't have left me.

How typical my beliefs and behaviors are of those who've grown up in alcoholic homes! The literature says that children of alcoholics don't know what normal is, that we are obsessive approval seekers whose identity is lost in the process, that we will go to any extreme to hold onto a relationship in order to avoid the pain of abandonment — even though we are masters at seeking relationships with those who will abandon us — that our loyalty to others is unparalleled.

What is normal for me is to feel responsible for everything that happens; it is my fault if things go wrong, if I am treated poorly, if I am lied to, abused. I know how to take responsibility. I do not know how to turn the hurt around, to set limits on how I allow myself to be treated, to say "no," to leave.

I have been masked for most of my life. The point was to look good, not what was going on inside. I learned early not to talk about what lay beneath the surface. I learned early not to know. Like others who as children had suffered the emotional abuse of broken promises and lies — lies that disguised the essence of our own reality and the context of our lives — I had thoroughly integrated the three cardinal rules of alcoholic homes: don't talk, don't trust, don't feel.

The lie masks personal shame. I look at my lovers and see how our lies mask our hatred of who we are...The lover of mine who turned all of her lesbian books with the titles facing the wall, so that no one would know who she really was...The lover who displayed all the right feminist and lesbian books to impress her more activist sisters...The lovers who so hated themselves, their own identities, that they could not face the truths about themselves that loving another woman revealed.

And how does this self-loathing project onto one's women lovers, onto other lesbians? How close is the anger, the violence, the rage to the surface of these veiled images we use to hide who we are? How much does our own denial and self-abuse hurt the women we love?

IX.
My mask splinters. Feelings submerged for years, stir. But there is nowhere safe to go for help.

Three brave and badly battered women sat talking to my mental health board members during an educational visit to the only shelter for hundreds of miles around. Moved by their courage to be so honest, so vulnerable with strangers, I felt oddly a part of their stories. My head battled with my feelings: I was, after all, not like them. I was a strong, political, assertive feminist. I was not helpless; I did have choice. And then, when they were asked the inevitable question, "Why did you stay?" my own dam broke. Tears surfaced. I felt sick and very small. I struggled to keep the mask intact, terrified of being found out.

I yearned to unburden myself to the shelter director or her head counselor for help, but as their local advocate with these conservative officials, I dared not approach even these women I loved. Besides my lesbianism was an issue; disclosure would have cost me my job. The tears kept welling up and the pain.

Now I see how we who have suffered these abuses in the past remain strangers even to those we know best. We remain strangers even to those we feel we know best. We remain strangers even to ourselves, locked into a glass cage that no-one sees.

Underneath my identity struggles with those three brave women was my unconscious belief that I was not like them — that I was not legitimate and did not count as battered, because I was a lesbian. Not only did I have nowhere to go for help, I didn't believe I deserved it.

X.
The pain of abuse with the women I have loved is the culminated pain of neglect and abuse from my childhood. ...She is a woman...That alone makes it hurt more...And I am drawn to that pain calling it love...

I learned young to hate myself. To deny and to repress what I felt, what I knew, what I wanted, who I was. I learned to be a woman in this culture, to devalue myself and others like me.

Like my sisters, I am a victim of the society of which I am a part, a society in which we have all been battered, crippled in our knowing of ourselves and each other. Even as I carry the wounds of a lover's beatings as physical badges of love, I do not hate her. I do not hate the women I have loved, do not hate my sisters, even though they may be different from me. No, I love those women who, like me, are struggling to transit the gap between what we learned about ourselves, what we suffered as society's victims, and what we dreamed of for our own reality. To hate, to reject my sisters, is to hate and reject myself. For how we treat each other is a reflection of how we feel about ourselves.

I am a mirror of the women I attract in friendship and love.

Each step that I take towards loving myself is a step towards loving my sisters; each step that I take towards loving my sisters is a step towards loving myself.

What we as lesbians believe does not guarantee that we will act in accordance with those beliefs and ideals. As visionaries of a world where women are safe and in control of their own lives, it is too easy to dismiss the distance between our vision and our pasts as insignificant. And yet, the very test of our vision is our ability to straddle that distance by acknowledging all of the pain and horrors it raises in our lives, in ways that heal the old wounds and prepare for that world that we so clearly see.

I stand on the fringes of our women's community watching with horror and sadness the self-hate we act out on ourselves and each other. I do not condone our violence. And I know that confronting our violence by embracing us all — those who abuse, those who continue to allow themselves to be abused, those of us who are party to either side of the violence — is to wage our own war, with love, against a society that would have us be different.

She Never Really Hit Me

Blair Northwood

The last time she assaulted me was several weeks after I had moved out. It was at "our" store, the local women's bookstore where we had met and had worked as members of the collective for the year that we lived together. There were other women around at the time — I had made it a point after I moved out to avoid being alone with her if at all possible, though she kept wanting to meet with me privately to discuss our relationship. So I was shocked that she attacked me there in public, in front of our friends.

The blow landed on the knapsack I was wearing. Some of her friends said that, of course, she hadn't actually meant to hit *me*. But it really knocked the wind out of me, physically and emotionally.

She left the store immediately. When I was sure she was gone, I went to my friend, Sandy, waiting in the car for me, and said though my tears, "What does she want? What does she want from me?" Sandy responded, "Does it matter?" and I suddenly realized that, no, it didn't matter anymore. What mattered was what I wanted, and needed. And I realized then that I had lived the last year as a battered woman.

Now, five years later, my understanding of this relationship has been filtered through many months of self-help support groups, workshops, talks with friends and my own work as a counselor in shelter for battered women. I have talked with many women who have experienced abuse as I had, some "much worse," some "not as bad." I now believe that, as women, many of us are raised in such a way that we are ripe for abusive relationships, and being a lesbian doesn't alter the values taught us, or the dynamics they encourage, enough to prevent the abuse.

I met her in the late fall, when I was a new member of the bookstore collective. She had been there for a year or more and seemed settled and comfortable in this community. Actually, after we separated, some of the women said they could have told me that I was in for some rough times with her, but they had chosen "not to get involved." I think I might have listened to their concerns — I had concerns of my own.

I had never been pursued as I was by her. When men had approached me with the intensity that she had, my guard had gone up and I had handled it by slowing down, backing off or leaving the relationship altogether, aware somehow that it wasn't what I wanted. But, as a lesbian, out only a little over a year, I found this attention much more flattering, more exciting; I believed it could lead to a relationship that I would cherish as I never had appreciated those I had with men. So I left myself open to the intensity, trusting my "sister" to be mindful of my needs and feelings.

Now I know that so many of the things I went through with her, the things she did, the ways I reacted, are typical of battering relationships. Then, I just felt I was doing something wrong. Even the counselor I was seeing at the time, an intelligent woman and a good therapist, didn't question the things I was telling her about our relationship. She didn't question how angry my lover got about small things, or the amount of energy I was obviously spending to avoid conflict and keep everything running smoothly. These behaviors and patterns are clear indications of abuse, but at that time, 1979, abuse wasn't a word that was spoken about lesbian couples.

The abusive tendencies were there from the beginning. To me, of course, they looked like love. Her pushing for sex until I gave in far sooner than I wanted; the jealousy she showed about my friends and my time away from her; the control she wanted; all these seemed, if not reasonable, at least acceptable expressions of her love for me. And she seemed so "right" for me that I really didn't want to lose her. She was all the things my parents would have liked in a man — upwardly mobile, slightly conservative, socially appropriate — and I was looking forward to a life with her that would match as closely as possible the "American Dream." And she was a feminist, as was I, so I knew we could put our lives together in a way that would fit the new world we envisioned.

But things kept happening that *weren't* right. Her irrational anger and her willingness to berate me, my assuming responsibility for her moods and my trying to control them, and her constant need to have me check in with her were all clues to me that *something* was wrong, but I couldn't put it together into a clear picture, a coherent statement of what it was or what to do about it. Even when I began working as a student counselor in a shelter for battered women, I didn't make the connection between what I was seeing and learning there and my own life. I still thought I just had to work harder or be better. I was aware that it wasn't all my fault or responsibility (though she was convinced it was), but the idea that there was abuse involved, that I was being battered, didn't occur to me until that incident at the bookstore.

Still today, when I talk about the abuse, I have to keep myself from qualifying the statement that "I was battered." I want to say "She never really injured me. She never *really* hit me. It wasn't *physical* abuse." But I was injured when, in my frustration over something she had done, I hit the wall and sprained my wrist. I was injured when my anxiety about how to avoid her temper, how to phrase a statement just so, how to convince her I had done nothing wrong, when in fact I hadn't, turned to shortness of breath and chest pains so bad that I went to a doctor. The emotional strain of struggling to maintain my self-esteem when she seemed bent on convincing me I was worthless was abuse. And it was physical abuse when she grabbed my arms to make me go with her, or to prevent me from leaving the room until she was through yelling at me.

There was also the psychological abuse of her raising her hand often to hit me, though the blow never landed until that day in the bookstore. I still don't know if the things I did or tried to do to keep from being hit were effective, or if she just didn't hit me. I was careful to watch for her anger, to stay out of her way, leave the room. I also learned that if I raised my hand or another object to her she, too, could be intimidated. It seemed to make her stop, if not out of consideration for me, then for herself. But I hated learning to use this tactic — not honest self-defense, but the same sort of bullying she used. It was what she finally understood best.

I had enough self-esteem — and support from friends — to know that I didn't have to live like that. She seemed devastated when I moved out, though she was already seeing someone else. The harassment I'd suffered while living with her continued when I saw her afterward, as she alternately played on my feelings and mistreated me.

After our last encounter in the bookstore, I knew I didn't want to be abused anymore. If I didn't have control over her actions, I at least had control over my responses to them. To let her know that I would no longer put up with her mistreatment, to express and affirm it for myself, and to maintain my own safety and distance, I wrote her a note, very to-the-point. I was finally certain that I wanted nothing to do with a woman who could be my lover, the person closest to me, and yet be willing to abuse me. Even knowing that, however, it took me months of processing, counseling, talking with friends and other battered lesbians to make enough sense of what had happened that I could go on to other healthier relationships.

The process of acknowledging, coming to terms with and accepting my abusive relationship so that I could move beyond it happened most effectively for me, as for most battered women, in groups with others like myself. Three of us who had been friends for a while connected on this issue. Linda said, "I've mentioned to others these experiences from my life, and no one responds. You and Barbara are the only ones who have seemed interested. We could probably all use some support. Let's get together and talk about this."

I had avoided speaking to many people about the abuse in the relationship. Most of my women friends either didn't understand at all, tried to trivialize it as though it wasn't that bad, or just couldn't believe my lover had acted like that and thought I must have "misunderstood" or be making it up for some reason. It wasn't worth the effort, when I didn't understand myself what had happened and why, for me to try to explain it to these women. And, of course, it hurt to relate these painful and humiliating experiences when no one understood. Though co-workers at the battered women's shelter knew I was a lesbian, I was terribly embarrassed not only to admit that I, a counselor, had been battered (I was still not making the connections between my own life and those of the shelter residents, and I thought I should have known better), but to let "outsiders" know what I was learning — that women batter, too.

Linda, Barbara and I met about three times a month for the next four months. Sharing stories, feelings, insights, fears and comfort helped each of us to acknowledge and learn from our experiences as we hadn't been able to by ourselves. We served for each other as support, sounding board and guide in questioning what had happened to us, what our part in it had been and what we could do about it now. We talked sometimes about including others in our group, but we didn't think the closeness we had developed would let others in at this point, and none of us was feeling particularly like a "leader," ready to start another group for others.

We did, however, want others to know that we were working on this. We wanted other lesbians, if their relationships were abusive, to know they were not the only ones and it wasn't their fault, things we had believed while we were with our lovers. We wanted to make what little information we had available to others. In August of that year, 1980, I attended a series of workshops on battering in lesbian relationships at the Michigan Womyn's Music Festival. That fall, Linda, Barbara and I gave presentations at two conferences in Denver: the Second National Conference on Violence Against Women, and Lesbians Colorado II, a statewide gathering of lesbians. (I had not realized that there had been a workshop at the first Lesbians Colorado Conference the year before. At that time I was with my abusive lover, and had not yet identified myself as a battered lesbian. That workshop had been a presentation of information gathered from counselors and therapists about the known incidence of battering among their lesbian clients.)

At those two workshops, we presented ourselves as formerly battered lesbians, gave background on how we had begun meeting and talked about our individual processes in coming to terms with our experiences. Then we opened the workshop to discussion from the floor.

Response to both workshops was similar. Participants wanted us to compare the lesbian experience to that of straight battering, they wanted to talk about their own experiences and they wanted to know if there was a group available for lesbians needing support. We had to say there was no group.

Diane, another formerly battered lesbian who had attended both presentations, was particularly interested in making sure that there was a group available for those women who might need it. We all agreed, but realized from our experience in trying just to meet with each other that we didn't have enough energy to do the work necessary to start a public support group. I told Diane that, if she would be in charge, I would provide her as much assistance as I could. Together, we started the RUTH Support Group for Battered Lesbians.

RUTH met as a scheduled group from February to November, 1981. During that time, we had a total of only about eight women meet with us, though we received calls and letters from others around the state, and even a few from out of state. I think there was only one meeting that five women attended; more often there were only three or four of us. Talking with others around the country who had tried to start similar groups we found the same thing — that the need for a support group was recognized, but that the response to the group itself was minimal. We never discovered why, exactly, more women didn't attend the group, but I think it was a combination of the natural reticence of battered women to self-identify and seek help and support, and the tremendous denial and need for education in lesbian communities.

Anywhere we spoke about battered lesbians, just as when the topic of "wife" abuse was first coming to public awareness, people did not believe it was happening, or thought it couldn't be very severe or serious. The responses were the same incredulity, jokes and offhand dismissal that heterosexual battering had received. In addition to the symptomatic denial, there was a general sense that, if "we" (lesbians) were doing the battering, we didn't want "them" (straights) involved. Getting help from almost any source — shelter, police, courts, parents — often means not only stepping outside the relationship, but also being forced to come out during a crisis, one more reason to deny or ignore what is happening.

During the time that RUTH was meeting, we circulated several flyers, offered two workshops through the local gay free university (only one person attended either workshop) and did an interview with one of the local women's papers. Unfortunately, we never kept records of how many calls we got or how women had heard about us; in any case, the response wasn't large. It was frustrating and disappointing to keep hearing that there was a need for a group, a need for information, and to have so little response.

Eventually, Diane and I stopped scheduling RUTH weekly. We didn't have the energy to continue to be available as a support "group" when we couldn't get or sustain attendance. We stopped saying there was a group, but made ouselves available individually for counseling (both of us were trained as counselors, in addition to having worked through our own issues), information, and referrals to knowledgeable and sensitive individuals and groups in the lesbian and straight communities.

I know the need for support groups and services specifically for lesbians in battering relationships is as great now as it was then. But in our state, as in others, there has been little or no progress by traditional resources in addressing this need. And, unfortunately, the awareness, response and support of the larger lesbian community has not grown significantly since the four of us struggled through our own crises to bond together and reach out to others.

As a lesbian, my abusive relationship was no different from a heterosexual battering relationship. As a feminist, my principles didn't protect me from the abuse, though they helped me to process it. It was as a woman that I was abused and as a woman that I have learned to value myself in my relationships today.

Nothing Is The Same Anymore

Mary Lou Dietrich

The fear still lingers months after my former lover attacked me. I live alone in an isolated cabin in the Maine woods. This is the land I love. This is the house I built with my own hands. This is the space my former lover violated.

She came here one March morning. We had just finished talking on the telephone — two painful conversations in which I said that our relationship was over. She said that we shouldn't see each other as friends right now, that a clean break was best. I agreed.

We had been lovers for about four and a half months. We are both college-educated, white, middle-class feminists. I grew up in rural Maine. She grew up in the big cities out of state. She had been married and has custody of two of her children. I have lived alone most of my adult life. As lovers, we lived separately.

That morning, she seemed angry on the phone, but I thought we reached a sane agreement.

About half an hour after the telephone conversation, a car slammed to a stop outside my cabin. I went to a window to see who was there. Before I could move to the door, she had kicked it open. She stomped in, shaking her fist and screaming, "I've come to break your windows. I've broken windows before, and I'm going to break yours." "No, you're not," I said and tried to steer her back out the door. "They crucified Jesus, too," she shouted. "There is no justice in the world. You're not a revolutionary. This land is not yours. It belongs to the Indians, and I'm going to come here with them and take it back."

I had seen her angry and threatening before, but still rational. When I realized that morning that there would be no reasoning with her, my heart froze in fear. I became obsessed with trying to save my windows — salvaged plate glass laboriously trucked through the woods and set in the casements. My windows and my grandmother's china — that's what I worried about.

I tried to push her out of the cabin. She pushed in. We fell to the floor. She straddled me and threatened to rape me. I was raped fifteen years ago in Cambridge, Mass., by two men, strangers. She knew the story, and she opened that old wound.

I couldn't get her off me. I screamed, "Get out of my space." Like a robot responding to a programmed command, she stood, turned around and walked out the door. I followed her and ordered her off my property. That just infuriated her, and she began to throw me around ouside. Finally, she got tired. Bruised and sobbing, I held onto her. I still was afraid she would try to break the windows. She started to caress me. This was worse than being thrown on the ground. Soon, however, the caresses turned into criticism.

I listened to her anger spew out. We stood there shivering. I was bleeding. I realized the only way to get rid of her was to calm her somehow. I took a chance and invited her into the house for a cup of tea. Over our steaming mugs, we talked about everything except what had just happened. I was scared and afraid to show it. I told her things I knew would please her. At one point, she looked at my injured hand and said, "I made you bleed." Finally, she left.

I freaked out. The house was a wreck. Outside, the screen door had been kicked apart. Inside, books lay strewn on the floor where they had fallen when we crashed into a bookcase. Tools were scattered where we had struggled on the floor. The place stank of her. At least the windows were not broken.

I needed to talk to somebody. I needed help. I tried to call several lesbian friends who knew both my lover and me. No answer.

I didn't know what to do. I felt filthy. I had felt the same way after being raped—not just dirty, but dirtied, as if I'd prostituted myself to my former lover just to get her to leave me alone. So I washed. I cleaned house. Then, propelled by outrage, I called the sheriff's department.

The sheriff's deputy wanted to know my relationship to my attacker. I took a deep breath and told him we were lovers. He didn't sound shocked. He was interested that she had been convicted of assault several years ago after she jumped a straight woman. When he explained that the process of pressing charges against her would mean that she would be served some papers, I became afraid. I imagined her hopping into her car and roaring over to my cabin again. I told the deputy I felt too vulnerable to file a criminal complaint. He said he understood and we hung up.

I still couldn't reach any friends on the phone. I had to talk to another lesbian. So I drove to see a friend living fifteen miles away in a cabin with no telephone. Luckily, she was home. She listened, she looked at my injuries, she let me cry.

The attack happened on a Thursday. By Saturday, I decided to go ahead and file a criminal complaint against my former lover. I thought that if I did nothing I would be condoning the battering. Somehow, my former lover had to be held responsible for her actions. Unless I took a tough stance, she would probably try to get away with terrorizing and beating women again. I was only the latest of her victims.

Before I began the process, though, I wanted to get a protective order from abuse. I felt so unsafe. I hoped a protective order would make her think twice before attacking again. But everything was closed for the weekend. I'd have to wait until Monday to talk to the authorities.

That weekend, I was very scared. I expected her to come back. I stayed alone in my cabin. I barricaded the door at night. I sat in the dark and waited and watched for her.

Monday, I went to the office of the district court clerk to fill out papers for a protective order. The clerk went into a small tizzy when she realized this was not a conventional case of domestic violence. She told me I was not eligible for a protective order because my former lover and I had not lived together. Desperate, I told her I needed some kind of protection. She suggested I talk to the district attorney. The secretary in the DA's office said I had to talk to the sheriff's department. The sheriff's department said the man I needed to talk to was not there. I should try calling him the next day. Panicked and weary, I wished I had accepted a friend's offer to come with me while I went through this process. It was draining to feel so vulnerable and unprotected and at the same time to have to come out to so many strangers.

Not until Wednesday, nearly a week after the attack, was I able to contact the appropriate deputy and file a complaint against my former lover. The deputy asked me why I wanted to take legal action. He told me to write a statement describing what had happened. He said the department could do nothing until the beginning of the next week. Nevertheless, it was a relief to talk with him. He took my story seriously, and he did not express any homophobia.

Five days later, he called me. "We brought her in," he said. "What?" I asked. "The DA's office decided to press charges," he explained. "You're safe now. Legally, she can't come near you or talk to you. That would be tampering with a witness."

I was shocked. Naive, I hadn't expected them to actually go to her house and arrest her. I was relieved, too. She would bail herself out, the deputy said, but she couldn't touch me again without serious repercussions. Some of the terror retreated.

In the meantime, I had told a few lesbians what had happened. Others heard via the grapevine. My former lover's closest friend expressed no surprise. "Oh, that's just the way she is," she said. "She'll be like this until she finds a new lover." Another lesbian kept telling me, "Don't be such a victim. You're acting like a victim." I got increasingly confused and angry.

Finally, I called the nearest battered women's hotline, operated by Spruce Run Association of Bangor, Maine. The woman on the other end of the hotline listened to my story. No homophobia. She let me be angry. No moralizing about how lesbians always should stick together. She helped me plan how to escape if my attacker returned. And she told me about a walk-in support group for battered women that meets once a week in Bangor.

I went to the group. I am still going. It has been helpful even though all the other participants are coming out of heterosexual relationships. "The feelings are the same," commented one of the facilitators after a session. "I was a little apprehensive about you coming here," she told me. "I didn't know how the other women would receive you. But it has worked out well."

The feelings *are* the same, I've realized. Those of us in the group share a sense of guilt (I must have deserved what I got), shame (how could I have got involved with the batterer in the first place?), shaky self-esteem (maybe I pick batterers to relate to; maybe my judgement is askew), humiliation (how can I face friends, family, the community after this?), helplessness (how am I going to rebuild my life now?), tenaciousness (if I can live through that, I can deal with the police, court, the welfare department, being alone), and rage. As one of the Spruce Run facilitators said, "Battered women are the strongest, bravest survivors I've ever met."

The response of the local lesbian community to the arrest of my former lover was demoralizing. Lesbians were upset — even angry — that I had called the police. "I can see turning in a batterer and calling the cops," said one woman. "But a lover? What does that say about your ability to be intimate with anyone?"

Another woman stated flatly, "I don't feel that you were abused by your lover or that she is your batterer." Several women put a lot of pressure on me to drop the charges. They said things like: "Oh, come on. Haven't you ever hit a lover? It wasn't all that bad." "You're dragging your lover's name through the mud. It was in the newspapers." "Do you realize that the state could take away her children because of what you have done?" They suggested setting up a meeting between my former lover and me. They volunteered to mediate so we could reach an "agreement."

I can think of few crueler demands on a woman who has been attacked than to insist that she sit down with her attacker and talk things out. I would guess that none of the lesbians who wanted me to do that would consider demanding such a thing from a straight woman who had just been attacked by her boyfriend.

These lesbians not only denied my fear, isolation and hurt, but even denied that I had been attacked. The lowest blow came when a friend called me the day before a pre-trial hearing. "You should drop the charges," she said. "We in the lesbian community take care of our own." "But what about me?" I asked. "Who's going to take care of me? Who's going to guarantee my safety and see that my house doesn't get trashed?" She had no response.

After the attack, I needed other lesbians to recognize how terrorized I was and how unsafe I felt. I needed other lesbians to realize that I was a victim of a kind of violence particularly hard to deal with. It came from someone who was once a joy and a delight in my life. I needed the community to acknowledge that my former lover broke the law. The attack was a criminal act. I wanted other lesbians to recognize that my basic rights to privacy and safety in my own home were violated.

I experienced so much victim blaming that I decided to write an open letter to the local lesbian community. I made copies of a statement on lesbian battering issued by the National Coalition Against Domestic Violence. I explained my reasons for filing charges against my former lover. She had made a choice to be violent, I wrote. She had thirty miles between her house and mine in which to reconsider that choice. Taking the case to court, I thought, was the most effective way to hold her accountable for her actions in light of her history of violence and her friends' unsuccessful attempts to deal with those episodes. I also paraphrased many of the comments that lesbians had made to me. I wanted them to think about what they had said.

Of the twenty women who received the letter, nine responded. Five thought the letter helped them understand what was going on with me. Three were incensed by it. One woman waved the flag of neutrality. Women I had considered friends did not respond at all.

I learned who my friends were the hard way. Those who stuck by me were essential to my sanity during the three and a half months before the trial. From March until the July court date, I agonized over the decision I had made. I felt bad, worthless, wrong. The week before the trial, I prepared to be tried myself. In my nightmares, I put myself on the witness stand, cross-examined myself and convicted myself. To help alleviate my anxiety, the facilitator of the battered women's support group suggested that I ask the district attorney's office exactly what they expected to happen in court.

I was referred to the witness/victim advocate. She was great. She took me into the empty courtroom and showed me where I would sit, where my former lover would sit. She put me in the witness stand. She looked up the name of the district court judge who would hear the case. She said she would be in court as support for me. "We have a strong case," she told me.

The day of the trial, three friends came to court with me. Their presence was really important. Two of the lesbians who had criticized my decision to take legal action were in court to support my former lover.

I hadn't seen my former lover since the day of the attack. Ironically, when she walked into the courtroom, I felt sorry for her and guilty for putting her through the trial.

Our case came up, and my former lover's lawyer disappeared into the hallway and huddled with the assistant DA who was handling the case for the state. Then the witness/victim advocate told me to go into the hall, too. There, the assistant DA explained that my former lover was willing to plead guilty of a charge of criminal trespass or nolo contendere (no contest) to a charge of assault. Criminal trespass would look better on her record, he said.

"I was assaulted," I said. "I want to stick to that charge." "OK," said the assistant DA, and we all returned to the courtroom.

My former lover was called to the bench. The judge asked her lawyer, "What is this case all about?"

The witness/victim advocate had warned me to expect my former lover's lawyer to make the assault sound like the result of passions of the moment — simply a lovers' quarrel. Instead, the lawyer covered up the relationship. "These were just two good friends," she emphasized to the judge.

Next, the judge asked me what had happened. Briefly, I described the attack. I was vague about the threats, and I did not say that we had been lovers. I was explicit about all that was in the written statement which the judge had in his hand.

Then the judge asked my former lover about seeing a therapist. Prompted by her lawyer, she agreed to see a court-approved counselor. The judge asked her about her children. She said that arrangements had been made for someone to care for them if she had to go to jail. The judge gave her a fifteen-day jail sentence — suspended. He ordered a year's probation with court-approved counseling.

It was over. I was relieved that my former lover plea-bargained to the assault charge, that neither of us had to testify against the other and be cross-examined. I was glad that she would get some sort of therapy for a year and that she hadn't been sent to jail.

Now, six months after the attack and three months after the trial, I have no regrets about going to court. I am angry and bitter that the local lesbian community doubled my victimization and continues to tolerate my former lover while it shuns me. Naming lesbian violence for what it is seems to be a taboo among us, the great breakers of taboo. Turning to the straight world for help — and thus admitting that lesbians batter lesbians — is high treason. Lesbian battering threatens to shatter our fondest theories about women, lesbians, ourselves. It shakes the fragile foundations of our communities.

My friendships that did hold up through the trial are stronger for it. I am very lucky to have three steadfast lesbian friends, the battered women's support group and a good therapist. Without their help and reassurance, I would not have had the stamina to struggle with being terrorized, betrayed and depressed. I would not have the courage to try to change my own behavior patterns, to survive this experience and to grow.

The Healing Comes Slowly

Arlene Istar

I have been trying for months to write these words. I want to write coherently so that you will be able to understand me, but my body is wracked with pain; I am nauseous and scared and weak.

The greatest problem I have faced in telling my story is to stop listening to her voice in my head. As I write a sentence I wonder what she will think of it; I still wonder if she will approve. I am still afraid she will find a way to silence me.

Silence.

I am not a quiet womon. The home we lived in together was filled with the sounds of two outspoken womyn, and two playful, noisy children. It was filled with opinions, and laughter, and anger; it was anything but silent.

Yet it is silence I remember most. I was silenced by her, and by my own confusion that robbed my words and thoughts. For months now I have been trying to write these words to break that silence. I write with despair, craving the truth. After living so long with lies, it is only the truth that eases my pain and isolation.

The violence I found in my life kept me in perpetual fear. My creativity had diminished; friendships were virtually non-existent.

During the two-year involvement I had with this womon I witnessed intense displays of rage, and experienced incredible physical and verbal abuse. I am still trying to understand what so attracted me to the situation and enabled me to stay through constant emotional degradation and threat of physical harm. I am still trying to understand how I survived.

Before I tell you my story, tell you what happened, I want you to know two things.

First I want you to know that I am an assertive and powerful womon. I do not fit my stereotype of a battered womon. I am telling you this because I *never* thought it could happen to me. Most lesbians I know who have been battered impress me with their presence and strength. None of them fit my stereotype. Do not think that what happened to me could not happen to you.

Next I want to tell you some of the good reasons I stayed. It is too easy to just trash her, to make her into an ogre, to discount her as a sick womon. As hard as it is for me, I want you to know some of the reasons why I fell in love with her, chose to stay with her through the violence, and still ache from missing her.

I fell in love with her because she was warm and loving and open. Her brilliance and clear political thinking dazzled me, as did her creativity — her artwork, her cooking, her carpentry, her ideas about raising children. Like me, she was Jewish and radical and understood the importance of making one's home in the country. She was responsive to our class differences in ways that surprised and delighted me. We had similar dreams of family and commitment, and fantasies of how we wanted to live. We often had hot, passionate sex. She bought me flowers, and chocolate, and crystals, and wool socks. She played a mean game of Pac-Man. She sang me love songs, and slow-danced with me in the living room. She did not do these things only at the beginning but throughout our relationship. Even when the violence was most frequent, she also expressed caring and tenderness toward me.

I want you to understand that I stayed with her for the same reasons any womon stays with her lover — because I honestly and deeply loved her, and was honestly and deeply loved by her.

I also stayed because I had nowhere else to go. I had moved across the country to live with her. My friends were 3000 miles away. Most of my friends eventually retreated, overwhelmed by my defensiveness and my unwillingness to look at the situation despite my chronic despair and neediness. I had no money. It was winter in the mountains. I was truly isolated. Through all the pain I could not ever quite believe it was as bad as it was. I stayed because I loved her two children dearly and because I had promised them and her I would stay. I could not bear to look at what I had become and staying seemed easier than facing the healing.

In the beginning it was only threats of violence. She yelled at me a lot, and if I voiced any concerns or didn't give in to her numerous demands, she would tell me not to "push" her. I was expected to take care of her, and the kids, and the house, before I attended to my own needs.

She had told me when we first met that she had battered her lovers. I remember feeling afraid when she said that, and telling her that I would leave her if she ever hit me. She begged and pleaded, cajoled and coaxed, yelled and demanded; she explained that I was not respecting her honesty and vulnerability. She convinced me I was being rigid. I didn't understand then that by retracting my limits I had given her permission to hit me.

The first time she hit me she said that I provoked it. She was angry at me because I was not wrapping the kids' Chanukah presents "correctly." The harder I tried, the more critical she became. I threw the scotch tape across the room and started crying. She walked up to me and began screaming at me, her face inches from mine. She repeatedly threatened to hit me. I finally told her to shut up and hit me already. She did.

I was startled that first time. I had little in my history to prepare me for violence of any kind, but particularly from another womon, a lover.

During the next six months (eight months? ten months? the time is still a blur in my memory), I was hit and slapped, often till I was black and blue. I was picked up and thrown against walls despite my chronic and disabling back condition. I was physically thrown out of the house in the snow with no shoes or coat. I had black eyes and fractured fingers. She destroyed things I loved. She would trap me, not letting me leave the room or the house or the car until the outburst was over. And if I could get out, where would I go, with no money and no car? Many times I ran out of the house and started down our country road in frustration and despair, almost grateful for her angry footsteps behind me.

In many ways the effects of the continual emotional abuse has been longer-lasting than the physical. There were "house rules" which included when to get up and when to go to sleep. If the phone rang late at night she would lecture me and my friends, telling them not to call any more. I was not really allowed to have friends because they took time away from her and the housework. She had a fantasy of creating a safe world for us: me and her against the world. Any relationship with others intruded into this private, sacred world. But the rules of our world were the ones she made. She would wake me in the middle of the night, screaming at me for the things I had not accomplished that day. She was furious at my physical limitations and would demand that I do work I was not capable of, offering to teach me skills like carpentry or plumbing or cooking, and spending the entire time berating me for my incompetence. I was told when to do the dishes, and when to make dinner. I was criticized for the way I drove the car, and the amount of dish soap I used. She told me I needed to do more than my share of childcare and housework to make up for all the years she'd been single parenting, although almost all of the eleven years she has been parenting have been spent with partners who have actively parented. She accused me of oppressing her as a lesbian mother. She demanded complete parental responsibility from me, and yet she retained strict control and decision-making power. She told me when and how to punish the kids, and resented any fun time I spent with them. She accused me of oppressing her as a fat womon, although I loved her body and when not in a rage she would say I was her staunchest ally in the struggle against fat oppression.

So many of her excuses for battering me were based on an intricate political logic, the explanations of which could go on for hours. Her twisted political analyses would serve as "proof" of my inadequacy, and therefore justified her rage and my punishment.

In the year I lived with her I can barely remember sitting and relaxing and reading a book. I was only allowed to do my own writing when she started to do her artwork. I wanted to go back to school, but somehow she went instead. I was not allowed to work, and then one day she demanded I get a job.

The violence came in spurts. At the worst it was an almost daily occurrence. It developed from the verbal sparrings of two articulate womyn into intense physical battles that left us both completely exhausted and physically injured. She was always loving and apologetic afterwards.

I thought that I could heal her. I thought, despite her history of violent relationships, that it would be different with me. And perhaps it was. She has told me it was worse.

I believe today that one of the reasons it was worse with me is that I fought back. Fighting back escalated the violence between us. It seemed to intensify her rage and her force against me.

In the beginning, I ran from the room when she hit me. It was to be our pattern, her yelling, my yelling, her hitting, and my running. She always came after me. Later our pattern changed and I refused to run or submit, and I began to fight back. My fighting back eventually became so furious that she began to run from me.

Toward the end I could anticipate her violent explosions. I developed an instinct for their causes and timing. Feeling the tension in the air, I would become prepared for battle.

I became so acclimated to living with violence that the only way I saw to get out was to fight my way out.

I am not a very physically powerful womon, but I became a formidable partner. Sometimes she increased her force, and sometimes she became paralyzed — she said it reminded her of being battered as a child. She began accusing me of battering her, although with only one exception she always hit first. More and more we were both equally injured.

I believe today that living with a batterer is akin to an addiction: it is believing the myths that things are not as bad as they seem, that things will get better, and that the violence, like the drinking, can be "controlled."

It is believing that your partner will be happy and cease her behavior if only you: forgive her, go to a couple counselor, have more sex, keep the house clean, cook better dinners, or make more money. It is believing that somehow your lover's violence will stop if you change your own behavior. These myths form the trap that perpetuates the cycle.

I would like to tell you I finally left the relationship because I became tired of being abused. But I think the truth is that I left the relationship because I was frightened of my reactions to her abuse. I was frightened to hear her car in the driveway, frightened to feel her rolling over in her sleep, and frightened if the grocery bill was too high. I spent days under the covers shaking, and in the closet moaning. I lived in fear of any sign of mood changes and geared my life toward placating her.

I was frightened of my own violence. Witnessing the fury I had become capable of was as frightening as her growing fear of me. I began to understand that we could permanently damage each other: that one of us, probably me, could die. Mostly, though, I just saw us living indefinitely with the violence.

What finally dented my isolation was when a womon in our community (an ex-lover of hers) gently questioned a bruise on my face. I lied to this womon, minimizing the truth of the violence. She, of course, was able to see through my defenses. My batterer overheard us talking (was she ever out of hearing?), and despite my having lied to protect her, she beat me on the way home. Yet this was the beginning of my finding a way out.

I left her not once but many times. In a two-year period, I moved back in with her three different times. Each time I pulled away, I became stronger. Eventually I found a job, bought a car, and began to set clearer limits. Our relationship actually became less abusive. If I could have found a way to stay with her and heal, I would have, but the damage that had been done to me was not healing as the violence decreased. I could not find a way to trust her and feel safe.

I do not feel good about the way I finally left the relationship; I left suddenly after an abusive incident — minor in comparison to others I had endured. I left with another womon. I do not believe I would have been able to finally leave without the support of my other lover.

The healing process has been excruciatingly slow. I have spent days inarticulate and afraid, days weeping uncontrollably. I am still afraid of her and of her power to manipulate me. She controlled my life for so long that I am afraid that she still can. I am afraid of all the people in my life who still keep contact with her — how can I trust them? Having lived in a rural community, to avoid her completely was to live in isolation.

I hear that she is healing, that she is trying to end the violence in her life. I desperately want to believe this. I want this not just for her, but for her kids and new lovers.

I envy, if this is true, her ability to heal. I wish I could just walk away from all this. I wish today I was not afraid of loud noises, people's opinions, or my gentle lover. I wish all my rocking and crying and raging and reading and thinking about political work would free me. But I am still just crawling through a maze.

Although the violence is gone from my life, the effects of living with violence are still with me. Today when I hear my lover's car in the driveway, or when she rolls over in her sleep, or when the grocery bill is too high, the old fear comes over me. I have no reason to be afraid of my lover but living with violence taught me to be afraid of anything sudden or different.

The pain and humiliation of living with violence went deeper than any other hurts I have ever experienced.

The violation of being abused by a womon I loved has shaken the very roots of my lesbian being.

I know that I will never again have the same unquestioning faith in womyn or sisterhood or lesbian utopia. I know in my heart today that we are all children of this violent patriarchy, and that our healing of ourselves, one another, and this planet is far more complicated than I'd ever envisioned.

This writing is really for:
> linda r., tree, micaela, bamboo, and laura d. — who tried to reach me
> clover — who did
> alixe — who helps me to heal
> and to my silver-bear who lived with the healing.
> Without all of you this world would be a dismal and drunk place. I thank you for believing in me.

PART FOUR

Lesbian Battering: An Examination

Barbara Hart

Definition of lesbian battering

Lesbian battering is that pattern of violent and coercive behaviors whereby a lesbian seeks to control the thoughts, beliefs or conduct of her intimate partner or to punish the intimate for resisting the perpetrator's control over her.

Individual acts of physical violence, by this definition, do not constitute lesbian battering. Physical violence is not battering unless it results in the enhanced control of the batterer over the recipient. If the assaulted partner becomes fearful of the violator, if she modifies her behavior in response to the assault or to avoid future abuse, or if the victim intentionally maintains a particular consciousness or behavioral repertoire to avoid violence, despite her preference not to do so, she is battered.

The physical violence utilized by lesbian batterers may include personal assaults, sexual abuse, property destruction, violence directed at friends, family or pets or threats thereof. Physical violence may involve the use of weapons. It is invariably coupled with nonphysical abuse, including homophobic attacks on the victim, economic exploitation and psychological abuse.*

---

* Please see a list of violent and coercive behaviors at the end of this article. These acts of abuse are illustrative of behaviors reported by battered lesbians to the author over the course of the last ten years.

A lesbian who finds herself controlled by her partner because of fear of violence may be battered even if she has not been physically assaulted. If her intimate has threatened her with physical violence or if her partner is aware that merely menacing gestures intimidate her because of a past history as a primary or secondary* victim of violence, the lesbian is battered who is controlled or lives in fear of her lover because of these threats or gestures.

In determining whether lesbian violence is lesbian battering, the number of assaults may not be telling. The frequency of the acts of violence may not be conclusive. The severity of the violence may also not be determinative.

Lesbian battering is the pattern of intimidation, coercion, terrorism or violence, the sum of all past acts of violence and the promises of future violence, that achieves enhanced power and control for the perpetrator over her partner.

Why do lesbians batter?

Like male batterers, lesbians who batter seek to achieve, maintain and demonstrate power over their partners in order to maximize the ready accomplishment of their own needs and desires. Lesbians batter their lovers because violence is often an effective method to gain power and control over intimates.

Lesbians, like their non-lesbian counterparts, are socialized in a culture where the family unit is designed to control and order the private relationships between members of the family. Men are assigned the ultimate power and authority in family relationships. This is true despite the fact that there is nothing inherent in the male gender which would render them the appropriate wielders of power. Rather, this attribution of "legitimate" power is given to men based on a system of beliefs and values that approves and supports men's power and control over women — *sexism*.

Roles in the family are defined based on this unequal power. A hierarchy of privilege, power and ultimate authority is established, with each family member being assigned a slot.

---

*A secondary victim is one who witnesses either the violence inflicted on another or the effects of such violence.

Family members constitute a discrete unit, separated somewhat from persons outside of the family. Individuals are treated like the property of the unit. Family members feel a strong connection of ownership to each other and expect a greater degree of loyalty and trust from each other than from outsiders. Intimate partners in family units believe that they are entitled to certain services from each other. They also feel that they have the right to exercise some degree of control over other family members.

Distribution of the limited resources of the family — energy, creativity, time and economic assets, to name a few — are determined by those most powerful in the hierarchy. Where there is a difference among family members in preferred utilization of the resources, those in power are able to choose among the several options. Critical and mundane decisions about the life of the family are also made by those persons, or the individual, holding the principal power.

Further, in this culture where many forms of violence are permissable — where violence often is not a crime, where there are few severe consequences for violence, such as incarceration, economic penalities, embarrassment or community ostracism — individuals may choose to use violence to enhance their control over other family members. Since violence is a tolerated tactic of control and is condoned within broad limits, particularly within the family, battering of intimate partners is widely practiced.

Lesbians, like non-lesbians, often desire control over the resources and decisions in family life that power brings and that violence can assure when control is resisted. The same elements of hierarchy of power, ownership, entitlement and control exist in lesbian family relationships. Largely this is true because lesbians have also learned that violence works in achieving partner compliance. Further, lesbian communities have not developed a system of norms and values opposing power abuse and violence in our relationships.

Which lesbian will batter?

Perhaps the partner who is physically stronger and perhaps not.

We know that part of the effectiveness of men's violence as a tactic of control is that their size and physical strength, compared to women, is such that men's violence has the potential to inflict serious bodily harm on women. Nonlesbian women will often acquiesce in the demands of the violent partners because of the knowledge that noncompliance may be followed by violent attacks that could result in injury.

But just as men choose to batter and also choose to not batter because they are physically strong, so also with lesbians.

The lesbian who is big, strong, an experienced fighter, or trained in the martial arts may represent a greater threat or danger to her partner than a woman of similar physical prowess. As well, a sharp difference in physical power may give the violence clout or persuasive power that would be absent if the partner were more physically equal.

Thus, one lesbian might choose not to be violent because she concludes that it would not work by virtue of her lack of physical power relative to her partner. Another could choose to be violent because she concludes violence will intimidate her partner and because she believes she can handle any violent response safely. Another lesbian with years of street or bar fighting experience might choose not to use violence to control her partner because she believes that it would be unfair and morally wrong. Yet another lesbian might choose to use violence to control by employing a weapon to eliminate her comparative weakness and to overcome the physical power possessed by her partner.

Thus, even though superior strength can render violence a more effective tactic of control, many choose not to use it.

Perhaps the partner who has more personal power and perhaps not.

Men who batter usually possess more personal power in their lives than the women they victimize. Personal power is based on education, income and economic security, employment skills and marketability, class, age, religious experience, physical power, health, social skills and networks, etc. Each partner possesses a particular amount of every attribute of power. Some attributes, like income or employment skills, may be more significant measures of personal power than others in any particular relationship. But men do not batter because they have more personal power than their partners. Nor do they batter because they happen to have less. Violence is not a necessary outgrowth of differential power.

Men batter because violence will usually give them immediate and total control over their partners, because it maximizes the power they have over the events of their family lives, because it feels strong and powerful to terrify the recipient of violence, and because there are relatively minor adverse consequences afterwards.

So also do lesbians batter. But not all powerful lesbians batter and not all batterers are powerful. Lesbians may choose to batter if they believe it will achieve the change or compliance desired of their partners, if they believe that coercive power is tolerably utilized in relationships, and if they conclude it is safe to batter.

Many lesbians who batter, regardless of their portion of personal power, demonstrate strong powers of coercion and intimidation, such that members of the couple's friendship network or their immediate lesbian community may defer to or pacify the batterer to avoid confrontation or humiliation.

Perhaps the partner who experienced violence as a child and perhaps not.

Many female children are physically or sexually abused by family members or friends as children. As victims of violence, young women certainly learn the power that violence grants. Violence can terrorize, immobilize and render fearful the most competent and extroverted, as well as the weak and powerless. Children, whether or not they are victims, observers or perpetrators, learn early that violence eliminates the recipient's control over her own life. Children learn the perverse pleasure they may derive from dominating others. Children learn that there may be few adverse consequences to violence. Children learn that parents or adults who espouse nonviolent, nonabusive philosophies may also batter and that adults sometimes behave very differently from the values they claim. Children who grow up in families where there is no model for negotiating over scarce family resources or for strategizing for maximizing the need and wish fulfillment of each family member, may lack ethical concepts of sharing and fairness and skills for problem-solving.

Surely, many girl children also learn that violence is not appropriate female behavior. Additionally, girl children who grow up as victims of violence often strongly reject violence as a tactic of control. This is particularly true for women who perceive the childhood violence as unjust and unnecessary.

Unfortunately, there is not any research data that answers the question of how many lesbians who were violated as children choose to be violators as adults. The fact that a woman was abused as a child is not a reliable indicator that she will batter her partner.

Perhaps the lesbian who is acutely homophobic and perhaps not.

All lesbians feel vulnerable and endangered to some extent because of the reality of the virulent prejudice and coercive, punitive power that has been brought to bear against us. To the lesbian who greatly fears exposure or self-hatred, an understanding of the risks of exposure may create a chronic emotional crisis where self-protection and self-validation consume exhausing amounts of energy.

The fragility of the control that lesbians can exercise to prevent exposure may leave the woman who feels highly at risk always in a state of at least mild anxiety. She may also be enraged that she cannot assure that her best efforts at invisibility will protect her. As a consequence, she may feel powerless — a pawn who can be hurt terribly at the whim or indiscretion of others.

Because of her vulnerability, the acutely fearful lesbian may expend endless energy to lead a duplicitious life — to act in the dominant culture as a non-lesbian and to live within herself as a lesbian. This expenditure of energy is enormous and continuous. It robs her of her best creativity and strength. It diminishes her. Often she may hate the system that oppresses her but also hate herself for being so vulnerable. But this does not precipitate violence or abuse of her partner. Although the lesbian experiencing homophobia or internalized homophobia copes with inordinate stress and rage, these do not override her capacity to choose to be violent. Nor does the fact that she lives in terror due to injustice determine her decision to act justly or unjustly toward others.*

Perhaps the lesbian who holds contempt for women or who identifies with men and perhaps not.
Misogyny is the hatred of women. A misogynist attitude is one that devalues, discredits or disparages women. Young women are taught in this culture not to trust or respect women, to believe that women are less competent than men. The media, purveyors of cultural norms and values, constantly reinforce this inferiority of women. It is, therefore, not surprising that women harbor contempt and hatred for women. Women who have worked diligently to be rid of self-hatred will never totally succeed in that endeavor in a society where women-hating is endemic.

Lesbians who have been battered often report that a seemingly integral part of the pattern of violence inflicted upon them is derogatory, women-hating tirades by the batterer.

Does the lesbian who uses women-hating verbal attacks as a tactic of control hate herself as a woman or does she hate other women, distinguishing herself somehow from them, or does she permit herself to ventilate women-hating attitudes because she knows this type of assault will be a particularly effective tactic of control over the woman she is abusing?

---

* It is often believed that oppressed people will explode with equally violent oppressive actions toward their oppressors when the opportunity and risks permit, displacing their rage at convenient and safe targets. This belief embodies the fear of the oppressors that retaliation in kind will occur if control of the oppressed is relaxed, justifying continued oppression. It does not accurately describe the response of the oppressed.

It has been suggested that lesbians who batter do so because they are identifying with men, the powerful gender. The process of identification with men is rarely a denial of the lesbian batterer's womanhood. It is not usually conscious self-hatred of herself as a woman. It may involve devaluing her partner based on her "lesser worth" because she is a woman. Sexually pejorative salvos may be used because they are most shameful and debilitating — most powerful. Identification may include an assessment that the lesbian batterer has the physical and personal power to batter successfully without adverse consequences — akin to men. It may entail a strong sense of ownership of the partner which brings with it the right to use her at will.

But identification with men or hatred of women does not compel violence, although it may allow the lesbian batterer to conclude that violence as a tactic of control will be successful or to feel justified in her actions.

Perhaps the lesbian who perceives herself to be victimized by the world and misused or controlled by her victim and perhaps not.

Most men who batter are said to feel controlled by people and circumstances other than themselves. That luck rules supreme and theirs is rotten. That disaster is more likely to befall them than other people.

Not only do male batterers describe themselves as the accidental or intentional victims of others' neglect or injury, they also see themselves as "henpecked" — controlled by their partners.

Lesbian batterers also express feelings of powerlessness and helplessness in their relationships and assert they are controlled and victimized by their partners. Lesbian assailants invariably utilize every disagreement by the partner, every failure to meet the batterer's needs, every independent/self-caring action by the partner as a violation or external control imposed by the victim.

Clearly, some lesbians who choose to batter are unjustly treated by persons and institutions. Some lesbians who batter are not in relationships with women who try to meet every expectation of the assailant. Many lesbians who batter are met with genuine adversity and hardship.

But there is no evidence to suggest that the lives of batterers are actually less rich or more fraught with injustice than lesbians who do not choose to batter. Furthermore, there is strong evidence from battered lesbians that they have persistently worked very hard to fulfill their partner's expectations and to nurture them through difficult times.

And many lesbians who meet with very trying circumstances and who are treated unkindly by their partners do not batter.

Perhaps the lesbian who has anger control or communications problems and perhaps not.

Many lesbian batterers speak of the inordinate anger that is generated by their partners. They acknowledge that identical behavior by another person would not propel them into the rage they feel toward their partners. Lesbian batterers describe themselves as angrier than other women; struggling hard to have some respite from the anger that is aroused by the partner. Sometimes the anger seems to come out of nowhere and sometimes it feels justified. There is no consistency about whether any particular attitude or behavior manifested by a battered lesbian will trigger the anger.

Batterers are not aware of the reasons behind the "triggering." They are often oblivious to the attitudes, beliefs and values that are the underpinning of the "triggering mechanism" that permit anger to explode sometimes even before they are aware the partner is resisting control or acting independently of the batterer's wishes. Lesbians who batter, like male batterers, strongly believe that once anger emerges, it becomes uncontrollable, and that violence subsequently erupts — the batterer having no control over either.

Battered lesbians report that batterers often appear to be looking for something about which to become angry to provide rationalization for battering. They also find that the batterer many times becomes angry only after she assaults to control and assault does not produce the desired compliance.

Whether anger is present or not, it does not eliminate the

batterer's capacity to choose violence as a tactic of control. That choice is fully hers.

Battered lesbians are often told by partners who have sought help from therapists not informed about battering that she batters because she is not adequately able to communicate her needs and feelings, nor able to express herself. She somehow short-circuits and becomes violent, with violence being a reflection of frustration, not a tactic of control.

Underlying this claim is a misconception that better communication would produce a better understanding of needs and feelings which would, in turn, result in the partner working harder to accommodate the batterer and violence being thereby averted. This assumes that the batterer is a person whose needs are not well understood and that the battered lesbian has a responsibility to go the additional distance to respond positively to the batterer's needs.

Both assumptions are often false. Many batterers are excellent communicators. Batterers who have worked in therapy to increase their communication skills, without first achieving the termination of violence or threats of violence, become more skillful, sophisticated controllers of their partners — better terrorists.

Many lesbians who are not articulate or do not have a clear sense of their feelings and needs are not violent. Most lesbians striving to improve communication skills and to better identify and actualize their needs and feelings have never considered violence as appropriate activity in relationships.

There is no profile of a lesbian batterer — no personal attributes or circumstances which permit reliable prediction or identification of the lesbian who will batter her intimate partner.

For a lesbian to choose to batter her partner, she must conclude that:

- She is entitled to control her partner and that it is her partner's obligation to acquiesce in this practice.
- Violence is permissable. (She can live with herself and conclude that she is an ethical/moral person even if she

chooses violence against her partner.)
• Violence will produce the desired effect or minimize a more negative occurrence.
• Violence will not unduly endanger her. (She will neither sustain physical harm nor suffer legal, economic, or personal consequences that will outweigh the benefit achieved through the violence.)

Isn't lesbian violence more often fighting than battering?

The notion that physical violence between lesbians is usually fighting in which both partners engage is false and gravely endangering to battered lesbians.

Certainly there may be lesbians who fight with their partners or relationships in which both partners assault each other. Many may prefer to think of the violence in lesbian relationships as trivial, nuisance behavior of little consequence. Perhaps it is because lesbian partners are often of similar strength and size, therefore seemingly incapable of inflicting any serious physical harm on the other, or because as women we have been taught that violence is not appropriate and have not learned to fight.

Battering occurs within all lesbian communities regardless of class, race, age and lifestyle. It is critical that lesbians not conspire in any effort that would trivialize the great danger and destruction in lesbian battering.

The definition of lesbian battering in this paper recognizes that there are lesbian relationships in which both partners (or in the case of nonmonogamous relationships, all lovers) participate in violent conduct toward each other. Even where this violence is repeated and a pattern evolves between the intimates, this violence is not battering unless the effect of the violent conduct is to render the perpetrator more powerful and controlling in relation to the recipient. This is not to say that the author is approving lesbian violence while concluding that lesbian battering is immoral, illegal, and damaging in contrast to the peaceful, egalitarian relationships valued by feminists. The author believes that lesbian violence or fighting is, similarly, damaging and endangering.

It is also not to say that battered lesbians have never been violent toward the women who have battered them. Many have. But the violence is largely self-defense and sometimes is rage at past violations.

Battered lesbians do not characterize the violence that occurs in their relationships as arising out of fighting that was safe ventilation, contests of strength or consensual. Battered lesbians describe the patterns of violence as terrorism and control as outlined briefly in the beginning of this paper.

A lesbian who has been battered often believes, as apparently do some therapists and advocates, that her experiences of violence at the hands of her partner were "mutual" since she may have knocked her partner down to escape from a room in which she was being confined or she may have violently ejected the batterer from her apartment after the batterer broke in or she may have picked up a baseball bat and threatened to assault the batterer if she approached one step closer or she may have in a rage beaten the woman who had been battering her.

A significant number of battered lesbians, when first seeking assistance from friends or from battered women's advocates, question whether they really were battered if they have acted violently even once toward the batterer. It is as if they have concluded that absent any violence they can with clarity identify themselves as victims of the abuser, but once they have been violent, especially if it has worked in the immediate situation to stop the batterer, they are compelled to see themselves as equally culpable — as batterers — and as obligated to fight back every time or otherwise to accept the ultimate responsibility for the battering.*

For many, the batterer has instigated and reinforced this

---

*There is no statistical data to demonstrate the proportion of battered lesbians who have acted violently to stop battering — who have fought back. However, many battered lesbians who have acknowledged violence in defense of themselves or others have suggested that immediately after separation from the abuser, they were confused about whether they had been batterers, as well as victims. Their understanding of violence and battering in the relationship had become tailored to the belief system of the batterer, and it blaming of the victim — this reversal of reality. Sometimes the batterer will threaten to report acts of violence by the battered lesbian to the police, pointing out that if the battered lesbian has acted violently to such an extent that she could be criminally liable, then she surely is not battered and has engaged in mutual violence. Sometimes the batterer points out that the battered lesbian has hit her in public, so that no one will believe that she is tyrannized in private.

Invariably batterers blame battered women for the violence they inflict — alleging that if only the battered lesbian had not provoked her, the batterer would not have been violent; that the batterer is really under the control of the victim, helpless in the face of her behavior, and compelled to violence.

Batterers always see themselves as the victims of the battered woman. This perceived victimization is repeatedly shared with the battered lesbian.

Most battered lesbians are ashamed of the violence they have inflicted on the batterer. Since all battered lesbians have engaged in extensive efforts to protect the batterer from exposure as a terrorist and from the consequences of her violence, battered lesbians may continue "taking care of" the batterer by blaming herself, maximizing her violence and minimizing that of the batterer.

Many battered lesbians are women of substantial physical prowess and power; women who are objectively very much more powerful than their assailants. They are women who choose not to use this power to control the perpetrator or would do so only to protect themselves or stop the batterer. It is particularly hard for these women to acknowledge to themselves and to others that they have been battered. The powerful lesbian may not live in fear of the violence of her partner. She may, rather, live in dread of the violent episodes and in anxiety about control confrontations. Even though not

---

took careful reflection on issues of control and power for clarity to emerge. Often this process took several months. Where the battered lesbian did not have the opportunity to think through her experience with a person knowledgeable about violence in intimate relationships, the recipient of battering sometimes found that the sorting-out and clarification process took longer.

fearful, she alters her life to accommodate the batterer and worries that her efforts will not suffice to avoid abuse. She may not fear the batterer's usual violence, but may fear that escalation in violent behavior could include suicide or assault on third parties.

Therefore, because a battered lesbian may have used violence against her batterer and because the batterer is convinced that the victim is responsible for the batterer's abuse, it is not surprising that many battered lesbians are confused when first contacting battered women's advocates to break free of the violence and to establish lives outside of the control of the perpetrator. It is not surprising that they may view themselves as both a batterer and a victim.*

Although it is critical that a woman who seeks assistance be afforded an opportunity to look carefully at the violence in her relationship to assess whether she is battered, it is imperative that she receive any emergency shelter and support services she requires and that she not be denied safe shelter during assessment. The availability of services must not be conditioned on the clarity of the caller.

This analysis of lesbian battering assumes that it is a rarity that a woman who is a victim of lesbian battering becomes a batterer later on in the relationship with the same person who battered her, nor is she likely to become a batterer in subsequent relationships.

The patterns of control and terrorism precipitated by battering are not easily undone. There would have to be an incredible shift in the power of the partner so that the battered lesbian acquires the power to use violence as a tactic to control and terrorize her mate. This might happen where the batterer becomes physically or mentally disabled and consequently loses the power behind the implied threat of violence.

Merely a realignment in economic security between the couple is not likely to shift power enough to make violence an effective tactical tool for the victim in controlling the batterer.

---

* What is tricky about this is that lesbian batterers see themselves as victims also. Meticulous interviewing should occur before conclusions are drawn about the admissions made by a lesbian that she is both a batterer and a victim.

Neither is the victim predisposed to use violence as a tactic of control where the power is shifted. Furthermore, it becomes even less likely that the power and the availability of violence as an effective tactic of control will continue to shift back and forth between the partners as the imbalance of power shifts.

As the battered women's movement, we should not reject the lessons learned about battering in non-lesbian relationships when attempting to understand battering in lesbians' relationships.

We know that some non-lesbian women who are battered by men are violent. The fact of their violence does not compel us to reach a conclusion that they are not battered. This does not mean that we as a movement have encouraged the violence of battered women. We have, however, supported and defended a women's right to act violently to protect herself, particularly where violence directed at her is life endangering. When men have said to us that the victims of their violence have been violent, we have not concluded then that violence was mutual or that the woman had not been battered.

Future work for lesbians and the battered women's movement

We have much yet to learn about lesbian battering. This paper, and perhaps much of this book, are only the beginning of our understanding about battering in lesbian relationships. Many questions remain unanswered. Much preliminary knowledge may require refinement, but as lesbians and as the battered women's movement, we must devote greater efforts and resources in order to assure that safe shelters and advocacy are available to every battered lesbian in programs that are antihomophobic and lesbian-empowering.

To learn how we may be helpful to the victims of lesbian battering and to effectively strategize to end violence in lesbian relationships, we must listen to battered lesbians. Just as we came to understand men's violence against women by listening to rape survivors and battered women, we must believe that our best and most reliable source of knowledge about lesbian battering is that which battered lesbians can share with us.

List Of Violent And Coercive Behaviors Utilized In Lesbian Battering

Physical

Assaults with weapons — guns, knives, whips, tire irons, cars, tent poles, high-heeled shoes, chair legs, broken bottles, pillows, cigarettes, poison.

Assaults with the batterer's own body — biting; scratching; kicking; punching; stomping; slapping; throwing down stairs; smashing eye glasses on the face of the victim; locking the victim in a closet or utilizing other confinement; tickling until loss of breath or panic.

Sleep interference; deprivation of heat or food.

Sexual

Rape; sex on demand; sexual withholding; weapons utilized or threatened sexually; forced sex with others; involuntary prostitution; coercing monogamy or nonmonogamy; denying reproductive freedom; physical assaults during sexual encounters; sexually degrading language.

Property

Arson; slashing of car tires, clothing, and furniture; pet abuse or destruction; stealing and destruction of property; breaking and entering; pulling out telephones; breaking household items.

Threats

Threats to commit physical, sexual or property destruction; threats of violence against significant third parties; stalking, harassment.

Economic control

Control over income and assets of partner; property destruction; interfering with employment or education; economic fraud; purchase of valuable assets in the name of the batterer only; using credit cards without the partner's permission; not working and requiring the victim to support the batterer.

Psychological or emotional abuse

Humiliation, degradation; lying; isolation; selection of entertainment/friends/religious experience; telling the partner that she is crazy, dumb, ugly; withholding critical information; selecting the food the partner eats; bursts of fury; pouting or withdrawal; mind manipulation.

Homophobic control

Threatening to tell family, friends, employer, police, church community, etc. that the victim is a lesbian if she does (or doesn't)...; telling the victim she deserves all that she gets because she is a lesbian; assuring her that no one would believe she has been violated because lesbians are not violent; reminding her that she has no options because the homophobic world will not help her.

Lesbian Victims And The Reluctance To Identify Abuse

Nancy Hammond

There is an ever-increasing awareness of the presence of physical abuse and violence in lesbian relationships. Those of us who work as therapists have learned that when we ask the right questions, and listen, some of our lesbian clients tell of being slapped, choked, cut, burned, or threatened with harm. Shelter workers get calls from lesbians needing a safe living space, free from the risk of physical abuse from their partners. We don't yet know how many lesbians are victimized, or what percentage of us perpetrate this violence, but there is no question that the violence exists.

Here in Minneapolis, many members of the lesbian community are committed to a recognition of the problem of lesbian battering. We are committed to understanding the roots of this violence, and to creating a structure within our community that offers victims safety and shelter and perpetrators safe alternatives to the abuse. This is slow, difficult work. Those of us who have not experienced physical and emotional abuse have often been unable to recognize and label the violence when clues of its presence and force existed in the lives of our friends or other lesbians around us. This paper will speak to the special issue of battered and abused lesbians, and particularly to their fear and hesitation in acknowledging the violence that they have suffered.

Since 1980, a Task Force on violence in lesbian

relationships has been meeting in Minneapolis. Through this Task Force, as well as through other outreach attempts by local agencies and therapists, efforts have been made to provide resources and support to battered lesbians. However, these attempts have been only partially successful. When efforts have been made to offer support and treatment groups specifically for abused lesbians, women have been slow to come forward. These outreach failures can be attributed partly to the difficulties of coordinating intervention efforts. More care must be taken in coordinating community forums and publicity with the beginning of new groups. This will allow women to name their abuse and victimization and to enter a program that is specifically designed to provide peer support. Clearly, the lesbian community must continue to provide education and outreach to victims that will facilitate their own recognition of their situation. For the healing to begin, the silence and shame must be broken.

Women's issues

This culture teaches women to be nonassertive, dependent on others for validation, and nurturers of their relationships. The recent changes and controversies about women's roles and rights have been greeted with mixed feelings by many. Both men and women threatened by the changes now being made frequently respond with increased fear and rigidity toward women, especially those women who challenge their assumptions. As much as some of us are committed to changing the way girls and women view themselves, at best we have grown up in a culture that is ambivalent about the empowerment of women. Many of us were told in families, churches, and schools that we were to be compliant, pleasing, and selfless. Almost all of us were taught to deny our anger by transforming it into depression, self blame, or bodily tension. We learned that our relationship skills, love, and caring were not only critical aspects of our value as people, but were to be used to join with, and take care of, others who might be under more stress or pressure. All of these teachings encourage us as women to believe that it is our responsiblity to do whatever is in our power to nourish and maintain relationships with others

— even in the face of physical intimidation and abuse.

For many years, people have written about the victimization that occurs to women within heterosexual relationships. Some aspects of these experiences are likely to be universal for abuse victims, and some will be readily transferrable to the particular experience of lesbian victims. For example, over the years we have learned that many battered women blame themselves for the abuse, accepting and internalizing the batterer's assertion that the victim is responsible, and that somehow the victim's behavior provokes the violence. Some women may be fearful of facing the contradiction that they have made a deep commitment to live with and love someone who could be both randomly and brutally violent. Women hope that their partner will stop the violence and may resort to denial or minimization of their abuse. When women do remain with a violent partner, they are led to a spiral of ever diminishing self-respect.

Traditionally, women have lived with violence from male partners because they saw no alternative. They most often have been financially dependent on their abuser. The legal system, from police officers to attorneys to judges, has been unresponsive to women's needs. The men running these systems have had a significant investment in preserving a family structure in which the man is in command, and the battered woman is viewed as a nag — provocative and hysterical. Male authority figures frequently have identified with the male abuser and the perceived stresses and pressures of his life, rather than with the suffering of the woman victim. Battered women have learned to doubt their own perceptions and sanity when physicians do not question a partner's statement that broken bones are due to a woman's clumsiness, when relatives look the other way at bruised faces and arms, when police officers tell the victim to "calm down" and send the male abuser on a short walk around the block. Often, when a woman reveals the abuse to a counselor, psychiatrist, or psychologist, she is given subtle or direct messages that she is both masochistic and provocative, that she has a deep psychological need to cause and then, inexplicably, enjoy, her abuse. With a legal and medical system that has been so male-identified with the patriarchy that heterosexual women experience a new level of abuse when they seek help, it makes sense that abused lesbians see few helpful alternatives available through traditional resources. When the combined obstacles of institutional sexism and homophobia confront battered lesbians, they may feel no choice but to remain in an abusive relationship.

Many other explanations have been suggested about why women remain in a relationship once their partner's violent behavior has undeniably surfaced. Some people believe that earlier family victimization leads women to believe that violence is a natural part of family life. Many women are influenced by male-identified religious traditions that teach women to accept male domination as part of the "natural order." Other women have been trapped in a double bind between living in an abusive relationship and risking something even worse. Some women hope that the abuse will "never happen again" and many others realistically fear an escalating cycle of violence, or death, if they dare to fight the abuse by calling the police, by initiating legal restraints, or by moving out.

Lesbian victims

As women of this culture, we as lesbians have also internalized many societal messages about women's roles. We need to be alert, questioning and helping each other to learn which of these roles to accept and cherish, and which to let go. The attention that we devote as a lesbian feminist culture to sensitivity, to processing problems, and to mutual emotional support, emphasizes our recognition of the value of many of the traditional areas of women's skill. Unfortunately, emphasis on these same values often makes the line between our responsibility to others and our responsiblity to ourselves a difficult one to traverse. It is critical, as we expand and explore our strengths as women and lesbians, that we continue to turn to other women for emotional support and constructive feedback. This process has been a very difficult one for the lesbian abuse victim. In addition to the traditional socialization messages about her role as a relationship nurturer, she has added conflicts and commitments as a lesbian (and often as a feminist) that support her reluctance to identify and acknowledge the extent of her abuse.

Lesbians often draw their emotional support from the lesbian subculture, and the number of women participating in a lesbian community often seems limited even in large cities. Many lesbian couples share close friends. When battering occurs, the battered lesbian is presented with a conflict about whom she can talk to. She may fear shaming her partner before the women who are the partner's friends, as well as hers. She may fear that mutual friends will take her lover's side, and minimize the significance of the violence because the perpetrator is a friend, and another lesbian. The lesbian victim who is isolated from other lesbians — because of geographical location, fear of coming out, or lack of knowledge about how to find other lesbians — is faced with far greater loneliness in her victimization. She may see her current partner as her only support system or her only available choice if she wishes to have a lover. She may perceive confronting the violence as a choice to live alone, with no other lesbian contact, for years into her future.

For most of us, it is relatively easy to spot male victimization of women, and to see the need for women to leave those situations where they are being abused by men. It is far more difficult for us to sort out our victimization of each other, both as women and as lesbians. We may believe that it is our responsibility, even as victims of abuse, to support our partners and to help them to change their violent behavior. We may fear that, as the truth of the violence is realized, mutual friends will totally reject us or our violent partner. We may hold ourselves responsible for labeling the ones we have loved as batterers, with this label following them, and isolating them from other women, far into the future. If we would prefer to remain with a partner who has been violent, and to work on those issues, we may fear that friends will tell us to leave the relationship, that it will never work out.

Ironically, we may be more tempted as lesbians to hold victims responsible for the physical violence they suffer. As members of a lesbian feminist culture, we support women's assumption of power. We take pride in our strength and fortitude as individuals, and in our ability to survive and grow even stronger. It is hard for our friends to see us, strong and tough-minded women that we are, as victims of abuse from partners who may be physically smaller. Paradoxically, even our friends might buy into the old stereotype that somehow, women aren't big enough or strong enough to really do each other damage in a physical fight. It is hard for us to acknowledge that a woman we love is capable of being cruel, violent, and brutal. We may fear to defend ourselves, believing that we are capable of inflicting far greater damage on our lovers than they are inflicting on us. If we do fight back to defend ourselves, our guilt may cause us to feel equally to blame, leading us to label ourselves as abusive. The shame from this may lead us to further secret-keeping and isolation.

Sometimes, the wounds from violence go beyond the physical and emotional levels, threatening the lesbian's spiritual integrity. Many of us have turned toward the reemergence and development of women-identified spirituality. We may practice this through a new awareness of natural sources of wisdom in the earth, seasons, and tides. We may seek to rediscover the Goddess that still lives through us. We may turn to ritual or psychic development that opens us to new sources of knowledge and realization, and also creates an avenue of vulnerability that reaches to the core of who we struggle to be. Our partner's violence may emerge even after we have opened ourselves in a very deep and spiritual way to each other. Some lesbians have felt cut off from their own spiritual lives when their partner has sought to harm them even through their openness of spirit. This harm may be done by physically disrupting rituals, by harming objects of spiritual significance, or by psychic efforts to abuse another woman as she opens herself spiritually. Although such violence may seem almost an abstraction to many women, difficult to grasp, to others it is devastatingly real. When we know what it is to be spiritually vulnerable, we know how tempting it is to deny that our partners may seek to hurt us in this way, too.

Homophobia clearly plays a role in the reluctance of lesbian victims to seek help. The controversies within the shelter movement about lesbian issues are now well known. Although many shelter workers are lesbians, they are often under pressure to stay in the closet to protect funding possiblities controlled by the straight community. Shelter programs have been designed for straight women, and shelter residents may be homophobic themselves. It is often difficult for those shelter workers who might reach out to the lesbian victim to do so because of the homophobia around them. Many lesbians would be horrified at the thought of calling for police protection, or arrest of their partner, an option increasingly more available to white heterosexual women. And lesbians are less likely than heterosexual women to turn to family members for emotional support in the aftermath of violence. Those who are not out to family members would have a hard time talking around the issue. Those who are out may fear reinforcing stereotypes of the "sickness" of lesbian relationships and lifestyles.

Financial problems can be a significant barrier to lesbians who want to physically separate from an abusive partner. For many low-income lesbians, going to a motel to escape abuse or living alone after leaving a violent lover are not realistic choices. Low-income women may be particularly vulnerable if they are also alienated from family members or other potential sources of financial support because of their lesbianism. Even women who are financially comfortable may be trapped into large mortgage payments, shared credit card debts, or other monetary obligations that would be difficult or impossible to meet on a single paycheck. An abused lesbian might be forced to give up a home, furniture, vacation property, or automobile that she helped pay for, but has no legal hold over or cannot afford on her own. Regardless of the victim's class background or present financial status, she may discover that in the course of her relationship, she has lost control over her financial resources.

As lesbians, we are continually challenging ourselves; learning new ways to be strong, independent, and yet loving and supportive to each other. Recognizing that lesbians are sometimes violent does not have to signal the end of a dream of a nonviolent women's culture. We have all grown up in a sexist and homophobic culture. The seeds of both victimization and violence are dormant in all of us. To realize the dream, we need to recognize those seeds for what they are, to expose them and gently tug them from the roots of our psyches, as they begin to sprout, take hold, and grow. For this work we need everyone's help.

How Homophobia Affects Lesbians' Response To Violence In Lesbian Relationships

Mindy Benowitz

As lesbian battering becomes more openly discussed, it is important to recognize the factors that affect our perceptions and responses to violence in lesbian relationships. This article focuses on homophobia's effect on lesbians in general, and on the particular difficulties faced by lesbian helping professionals and shelter advocates.*

Homophobia can be defined in two ways. It is a fear or hatred of lesbians and gay men, and it is also a fear of getting close to someone of your same gender. Like other oppressions such as racism and classism, homophobia directly affects everyone by producing isolation and separation among groups of people. We are taught that lesbians are totally different from "normal" women, and therefore considered bad. Homophobia is rooted in sexism, in that it is used to keep women "in their place." The word "lesbian" is used as a psychological weapon against any woman who deviates from societal sex-role expectations. Homophobia gives negative power to the word "lesbian"; to the extent that the label "lesbian" has power over us, it scares all women — both lesbian and non-lesbian — from exercising all of our human rights and talents, and thus maintains the status quo in society.

---

*The ideas in this article reflect discussions with members of the Minneapolis/St. Paul Task Force on Violence in Lesbian Relationships.

It is a truism that oppressed groups internalize their oppression. Members of oppressed groups grow up hearing negative myths about themselves and are treated in a prejudicial manner. They come to believe that somehow they must deserve the oppression they have received, and that the myths must be true. Since homophobia permeates society, lesbians have internalized the lies and stereotypes motivated by homophobia.

Individually and collectively, we, as lesbians, struggle to affirm for ourselves the beauty of women loving women. To encourage self-acceptance, many of us contend that lesbians are better than other people. This is a common reaction to being oppressed for our "differentness." We say that we do not have to contend with power issues, that we know how to have egalitarian relationships. We believe we are somehow able to sidestep many snags seen in heterosexual relationships. These beliefs of lesbian superiority have been important in reclaiming and building a sense of pride and value in ourselves. Contributing to our espousal of lesbian superiority is our experience, which may suggest that lesbian relationships and lifestyles can be more satisfying than our heterosexual relationships.

However, we need to realize how our "lesbian utopia" notions can backfire on us. We may tend to set different (higher) standards for lesbians than for others. We are reluctant to acknowledge that our relationships may not be so much better than heterosexual relationships. In reality, we too have learned about violence and power struggles growing up in this world. The belief of lesbian superiority carries a reactive tone of justifying our existence to a homophobic and hostile world. Thus, our homophobia leads us to perceive that lesbian battering is nonexistent or minimal.

Homophobia's root in sex-role stereotyping creates further difficulty for lesbians dealing with battering. For example, a myth exists that lesbians are not "real" women and want to be men. Many lesbians react to such stereotypes by attempting to choose among traditionally defined male and female sex-roles. Lesbians struggle against being too much "like a man" or too much like a "stereotypical woman," while fighting shame for being different as a lesbian in a heterosexist world. Our unrealistic standards make it difficult to admit that lesbian battering exists. We may condemn ourselves for being violent "like a man" or for allowing ourselves to be victimized "like a heterosexual woman."

Lesbians' silence about battering also reflects an acute awareness of societal homophobia. We fear fueling society's hatred and myths by speaking openly about lesbian battering. We fear hostile responses from police, courts, shelter, or therapists. Consequently, we are hesitant to call the police, seek counseling, or write articles. Speaking about violence or seeking help is an especially terrifying prospect for lesbians who need to remain closeted.

Lesbian shelter advocates and psychotherapists are beginning to facilitate positive changes by providing informational programs, support groups, and counseling for lesbians in violent relationships. However, internalized and societal homophobia may prevent lesbian mental health professionals from using their full potential to help reduce lesbian battering. Lesbian helping professionals face stresses inherent in being on the forefront of the battle to gain recognition and support for the lesbian battering issue. Many of us are unable to be open about our lesbianism with employees and co-workers, and fear that speaking about lesbian battering would force us out of the closet. Even advocates and therapists who are "out" often have difficulty bringing up the issue of lesbian battering and keeping it alive. Employers, colleagues, and funders often discount identified lesbians who regularly bring up lesbian issues. Many organizations that employ openly identified lesbians have only one such employee on staff. Given organizational resistance, it is difficult for us to maintain the courage and morale needed to continue to press for crucial services.

Shelter advocates face the particularly discouraging homophobia that is rampant in organizations of women helping other women. Lesbian shelter staff have been pressured to be closeted, have had their work invalidated, and have been denied promotions. Many have watched with frustration and fear as their co-workers abandoned them in response to the lesbian-baiting of funders, shelter residents, and community organizations.

Societal and internalized homophobia present additional difficulties for lesbian therapists and shelter advocates. We often feel a need to present a "together lesbian" image, so as to promote acceptance of ourselves and of the lesbain communities we are seen to represent. We may hesitate to acknowledge violence in lesbian relationships, wanting to protect our own images as well as that of the lesbian community.

There are ways to help us contend with the discouraging dynamics of homophobia. First, activities that strengthen our self-image and confidence as individual lesbian women will help us cope collectively with homophobia. Secondly, joining together in task forces and discussion groups on lesbian battering can be invaluable to maintaining morale. Also groups are generally more powerful and effective tools to affect community-wide change. Thirdly, nearly all the progress to date concerning lesbian battering is due to the efforts of lesbians. Without the energy and support of non-lesbians, it will be impossible to provide the services needed to adequately address the lesbian battering issues. It is crucial that both lesbian and non-lesbian women work to reduce homophobia and internalized oppression. With less homophobia, lesbian battering will be viewed in a more realistic light, and the battered women's movement and the lesbian communities can work together to help reduce violence in lesbian relationships.

Two Workshops On Homophobia

Suzanne Pharr

In 1982, when I became chair of the National Coalition Against Domestic Violence Lesbian Task Force, I was instructed by that group to create a workshop on homophobia for use in the battered women's movement, since it had become clear that lesbians working in the movement did not have safety or job security because of their sexual identity. There was little talk at that time about lesbian battering, and much about lesbian-baiting. However, by the time the homophobia workshop was in use for a year we began to hear more about lesbian battering and the difficulty battered lesbians had in finding safety or services within our movement.

In the summer of 1983, Barbara Hart and I met in Minneapolis, and with some trepidation planned the NCADV Violence in the Lesbian Community Gathering in Washington, D.C., for September of that year. Over one hundred women attended, told their stories of lesbian battering, and felt the pain of realization of how much more extensive lesbian violence might be than we had thought. It was then that we all began the search for ways to work with batttered lesbians, to provide safety, services and support.

This anthology is one of the many responses to the need we learned about in Washington in 1983. Other responses have been the development of lesbian battering support groups, task forces, and service delivery groups around the country.

Workshops have been given at local shelters and at state and national conferences. Articles have been published. Research has been done.

Yet we are still at the very beginning of our discovery about lesbian violence. Or how race or class or physical disability figure into the violence in lesbian relationships. There is much to be learned.

Here are some of the questions I'm frequently asked by people working with battered lesbians:

1) Don't you think that with women the violence is more often mutual?

2) Should we work with the battered lesbian and her abuser together?

3) Should we assume the violence is the same as heterosexual violence with the same dynamics?

To answer these questions I think we have to rely upon what we have learned from working with battered women these last ten years. Our first answer is that we must always work with women for their empowerment. We must listen to their stories, believe in their lives and their ability to take charge of them. Our work is not to help women; it is to support their empowerment.

1) There are those who believe in mutual battering, both among lesbians and non-lesbians. I am not among them. When one works with the complexity of relationships and the layers of truth in a life, one sees the surfacing of an imbalance of power in violent relationships, a greater need or will or ability to dominate and control on the part of one partner. To deny this difference is to trivialize the battering or to risk adding to the disempowerment of the abused.

2) Those people working with battered women who believe in putting the battered woman and the abuser (and often the sexually abused child) in the same room together

for therapy somehow believe that there is equal power in the world, and these same people, when working with battered lesbians, will want the abused and the abuser to sit down together. This arrangement always has semed to me to put the relationship above the importance of the individual and the empowerment of the abused woman.

3) There is an important difference between the battered lesbian and the battered non-lesbian: the battered non-lesbian experiences violence within the context of a misogynist world; the lesbian experiences violence within the context of a world that is not only woman-hating but is also homophobic. And that is a great difference.

The workshops on homophobia and internalized homophobia were developed to address that difference. We cannot begin to understand the effect of the homophobic world upon lesbian violence until we examine internalized homophobia. And lesbians cannot receive acceptable supportive services from shelters and anti-violence programs that are homophobic and unsafe for lesbians; therefore, domestic violence programs throughout the country must work on their homophobia before they can begin planning to work with battered lesbians.

These two workshops, then, represent a two-pronged organizing strategy. The homophobia workshop is to be presented by visible and safe lesbians (or very politically evolved non-lesbians) to the greater community of domestic violence workers, and the internalized homophobia workshop is to be presented by lesbians (who don't have to be visible in the larger community) to lesbians within the lesbian community in confidentiality and safety. We have to work on both fronts to free ourselves from violence.

Internalized Homophobia
(Oppression) Workshop

Note for Workshop Leaders

This workshop is designed for lesbian groups of ten to twenty women. It can be used for organized groups of lesbians, as a workshop for lesbians at retreats or conferences, or for a small group of friends gathered together in someone's living room. Its purpose is to open up the discussion of internalized homophobia, to be a beginning. It is a discussion that should be directed toward further action. In the end, each of the strategies for working against internalized homophobia can be used for continued organizing.

Sections I through IV are introductory and should be covered with speed. Sections V and VI are the heart of the work and should be given the majority of the allotted time. The workshop requires a minimum of four hours.

It is crucial in presenting the workshop that a commitment of confidentiality be gotten from the group. For many it will be the first time they have discussed how painful it can be to live as a lesbian in a misogynist, homophobic world. Be sure to offer a closure that acknowledges the feelings expressed during the workshop, affirms our belief in ourselves, and offers our vision of hope for the future.

I. Introduction to the Workshop

The workshop is about setting ourselves free, about loving ourselves and each other, about personal growth and political organizing.

The need for the workshop: homophobia, both external and internal, keeps us from being free. It makes us choose invisibility — closeting — which then makes us unable to know all of us, our numbers; unable to work together in our own behalf for our own rights; and unable to get the support of non-lesbians because they don't know we are lesbians. Homophobia can lead to our hurting ourselves and hurting others.

In order to survive personally and collectively, we must

break free of the restraints and damage of homophobia. We must free ourselves to organize for survival.

Group Work: Introductions — each person states briefly what brought her to the workshop.

II. Definition of Homophobia

Homophobia (meaning fear, dread, or hatred of homosexuals) is the result of a carefully designed system of stereotypes, myths and half-truths that serve to enforce traditional sex-role stereotyping which in turn serves male dominance. When women and men break from that system of male dominance (by loving the same sex, by exhibiting behavior that is out of line with traditional sex-roles), then homophobia is used as a weapon to draw them into line, and it works against both those who are gay and lesbian and those who are not. The threat of being called a faggot or lesbian keeps many heterosexual men and women exhibiting traditional stereotyped sex-role behavior even when they want to be free of it. Who wants to risk the weapons of homophobia — violence, ostracism, loss of job, children, family, church, community? Who among us can live easily without these things?

Group Discussion: Ways we enforce traditional sex-roles, beginning early childhood.
Examples:

1) What are the conventional expectations of female children?
2) Why is it that around puberty children begin calling each other "queer" or "faggot"?

III. Internalized homophobia

It is sometimes difficult to separate external and internalized homophobia. The gay and lesbian population has justified fears about the uses of homophobia against us: loss of families, jobs, children, homes, lives. The separating line comes when we individually and collectively come to believe that others are justified in their prejudices, when we believe there is something wrong with us, when we feel we do not deserve equality and freedom, when we take in the world's view and suffer from low self-esteem and self-hatred.

How Homophobia Becomes Internalized

A. Since we first drew breath, we have received messages of homophobia because it pervades every institution.

Group Discussion: With the exception of those institutions created by the gay and lesbian community, can you name institutions that support and nuture and offer us full legal equality, social equality?

Discuss each of these briefly:

1) the criminal justice system (how many lesbian mothers win custody of their children?)
2) schools (how does education promote homophobia?)
3) military
4) churches

B. Many of our messages have come from two major sources: education and the media.

Group Discussion: Examine the messages and images we have received from the media and how they have worked.

Examples:

1) What are the images of lesbians you saw as a young girl on TV or in books?
2) If the media is a vision of society, where are you in it?

C. Myths and stereotypes are created to feed and sustain homophobia.

Group Discussion: List and discuss myths and stereotypes about lesbians.

Examples:

Lesbians are man-haters; lesbians had bad experiences with men; lesbians are child molesters (See Section III of homophobia workshop for longer explanation.)

IV. Survival Against the Odds

What we must remember throughout this workshop is that despite living in a homophobic world, we gay and lesbian people keep on being, keep on going. We are all miracles of survival and should be proud of it. It is painful to talk about internalized homophobia but we must, in order to free ourselves from it. Many of us suffer from it to some degree. Those who are the most free are those who have worked hard to remove it from their lives. To remove it, one must first develop a consciousness of it.

V. Manifestations of Internalized Homophobia

Group Work: List as many manifestations as possible. Examples:

Alcohol and drug and food addiction; invisibility, closeting, passing; self-blame; not identifying with other lesbians; depression; destructive relationships; not working toward one's full potential, etc. Afterwards, have a short discussion of how people are feeling about the list because it can be depressing for some to look at so many negative results of homophobia at once.

VI. Strategizing for Freeing Ourselves from Internalized Homophobia

Group Work: List as many strategies as possible. Examples:

Set personal freeing goals; develop our own good, life-promoting institutions; develop political action groups; develop support groups, etc.

Choose several strategies and break up into small groups of six to eight people for thirty minutes to discuss concrete steps for ways to accomplish these strategies. Each group should name a facilitator and a recorder and write all the steps for each strategy on butcher paper. All steps leading up to the accomplishment of the strategy and those following it should be listed — i.e., if the subject is forming a support group to discuss sexual dysfunction, what are all the steps necessary before the group ever meets and what are the steps necessary for its maintenance and continuation? After these discussions, everyone returns to the large group and reports back. This is an important section because it will form the basis for community organizing and action.

VII. Closure

Two rounds, with each participant speaking:

A. Name one thing that helps you survive.
B. Share one thing you will now do for yourself or other lesbians.

A Homophobia Workshop*

Phobia, from the Greek, means fear, dread, hatred. For our purposes when we talk about homophobia, we are talking about that particular blend of all of these things that work to keep homosexuals as a hidden (closeted) underclass of society, discriminated against, treated as deviants, sinners, maliciously perverted, sick and abnormal. From those who hate us most, we receive the messages that we should be cured or killed; from those who are liberal and tolerant, we receive the messages that we must be quiet and invisible. This workshop is designed for use with the second group, those people who do not call for our physical deaths but kill us bit by bit with their demands for our invisibility, for our public denial of who we are and how we live. It is they who accept our outstanding work for social change in organizations for women, for peace, for the environment, within organizations for social workers, teachers, psychologists, and then tell us in return that they do not want our visible presence, especially when we organize to work against our own

*Developed by Suzanne Pharr for the Lesbian Task Force and Caucus of the National Coalition Against Domestic Violence. This workshop may be copied and distributed. Please give credit to the Lesbian Task Force of the National Coalition Against Domestic Violence. September 1983. Revised September 1985.

lesbian oppression, because they say that our lesbian visibility will hurt the organization's funding, credibility, or effectiveness in the community it serves.

For us as lesbian/feminists, such attitudes have been the source of much pain and confusion and anger. Clearly, it has been sometimes easier for us to take the brutality of the greater world than the subtle oppression of non-lesbian feminists, well-meaning in their sincerity when they say to us that we must consider the greater good, that the particular social change project, so endangered anyway, must be saved above all else. These are the women we love as sisters, these are the social change projects we helped create, that we bravely led, these are the only places where we thought there was a chance for us to flourish and grow, uncloseted and visible, and supported by loving women struggling for the transformation of the world. So, this workshop is for those people who say to us, "We don't see why you would want to endanger our work with your need to be so obvious. It's only a bedroom issue, and we don't care who you sleep with. All we ask is that you be discreet." And our answer is this:

What you see as only a bedroom issue is all of our lives, who we are, and what we live and die by. And we cannot live without our lives.

The Lesbian Task Force of the National Coalition Against Domestic Violence has felt a need for a homophobia workshop that could be used to address the homophobia in battered women's projects — among staff, volunteers, battered women, boards — and state coalitions and feminist organizations. Over and over we have heard stories from lesbians working in these organizations who were forced, upon the threat of losing their jobs, to be completely closeted, or, at best, so discreet about their lives that at every moment some decision had to be made about how much of one's real life could be shown. Also, there were stories of discrimination toward battered lesbians coming to a shelter for safety and finding it was not a safe place for them. Lesbians have told us stories of how their work is invalidated, of how they are kept from advancement, of the many, many subtleties of discrimination and oppression.

These are the stories of brave women who have stayed with their work, even when psychologically batttered and unsupported, and these are the stories of lesbians who have been fired, usually for some smoke-screen reason, and have grieved for the loss of their life's work. We honor these many women through this workshop.

The design of this workshop is drawn from the experiences of many women who have worked to eliminate homophobia in the workplace, in schools, and in feminist organizations. We are indebted to them for their work and great courage. With some modification, this workshop can be used for any group, though what is presented here is created mainly for the battered women's movement. It falls into two parts: the first is consciousness-raising about what it feels like, what it means to be a lesbian, and what forms discrimination takes; the second is more specific, seeking strategies for dealing with homophobia within the workplace or organization. Ideally, an entire day is necessary for the workshop; however, it can be squeezed into two-and-a-half or three hours.

One final note: This workshop deals primarily with homophobia as it affects lesbians and our lives; it does not treat the subject of gay men. This is a conscious choice on my part, for I feel that even though we share some common problems, nevertheless there are great differences, and for the sake of clarity as well as politics, the focus in this instance should be kept on lesbians.

The Lesbian Task Force is committed to discussing racism as part of all its discussions of homophobia. Parallels of oppression can be drawn throughout the workshop.

PART ONE

I. The Power/Privilege Chart

It is important to begin with a discussion of how oppressions are connected, of how homophobia is not isolated in its development, and of how similar it is to other forms of oppression. I usually begin with this chart on a chalkboard:

Power/Privilege The Norm	The Unempowered The Other
Men	Women
Rich	Poor
White	People of Color
Christian	Jews, Moslems, Atheists, all other
Heterosexual	Homosexual
Temporarily able-bodied	Differently abled
Young	Long-lived
Traditionally educated	Self-educated
Owners, managers	Workers
Adults	Children

Participants may add other groups to this list.

When one looks at this chart globally, the obvious question arises: How do the people in the lefthand column, who are fewer, control those on the righthand column, who are the majority? The participants will give many answers to this question and usually cover the issue thoroughly, but if they do not, here are some points to include:

1) Discuss how those who have power control

a. economics, resources

b. the criminal justice system, all the way from local police departments to the Supreme Court and Congress (Who, for example, is Congress made up of?)

c. education — Who does education serve? Whose history, culture is taught?

d. media — Who does the media reflect? If it is a mirror of society, who do we see when we hold that mirror up to our faces, which may be female, of color, or homosexual?

2) Discuss the philosophy of scarcity — that there are not enough resources and money to go around and therefore those who *have* must unite to keep the poor from taking their jobs, homes, etc. However, there are obscene profits being made, and we live with such statistics as those presented at the United Nations End of the Decade of Women Conference in Nairobi, Kenya: that women do seventy five percent of the world's work, receive ten percent of its pay, and own one percent of its property.

3) Discuss the use of violence as the primary means of control.

4) Discuss the seduction of the righthand column by the lefthand column. The lefthand column sets the norms, controls the most power; those on the righthand column are told through our institutions that if they "do right," then they will be let into the circle of power and privilege. What is not told is that there are very few openings for crossovers, and those who do get accepted are those who make themselves most "acceptable," e.g., gay and lesbians who *pass;* people of color who adapt most readily to the white culture, etc. This lure of achievement also sets up competition for the few openings available and pits us against one another. The same competitiveness occurs with our organizations: funders offer a little pot of money and we are told to go for it; we all struggle over turf issues, etc.

Ways to work against this power and dominance

1) Most people fall on both sides of the chart. For instance, one might be female, poor, and lesbian, but also white. What we must remember is that we have the *choice* of where we identify: in this example, the woman has no choice about being white, but she does have a choice about where she puts her life — where she lives, who she works with; she can put her life in solidarity with those in the righthand column.

2) Instead of allowing ourselves to be pitted against each other, we can make coalitions through common cause and solidarity — from a place of group identity and strength.

3) To fight the negative images of the media and educational institutions which cause internalized oppression, we can support and nurture our own culture and build strength within our own identity as gay and lesbians, as people of color, etc.

4) And finally, those who are in the lefthand column rarely, if ever, willingly yield up power to those on the righthand side. Power and rights have to be won or taken. For instance, very few people were concerned about the differently abled in this country, about how people in wheelchairs could not enter public buildings, go to public schools, or use public bathrooms, until a strong coalition was built and legislators got the experience of spending a day strapped to their wheelchairs. White people felt little concern about the lack of civil rights of blacks until people bonded together to form a movement and, among other things, whites felt the potential economic impact.

Others participating in the workshop will draw many more ideas from this chart, and they may add other categories of power and dominance.

II. Names

Ask the group to give all the names they have ever heard homosexuals called, and list them for the group to see. This is a good ice-breaker, for it gives people a chance to say the unspeakable, and to get out some of their homophobia in an acceptable way. There is usually a sense of the ridiculous and lots of laughter. This is also a time that names gay men are called can be included and general homophobia discussed. Here are some of the names people may give:

Butch	Bulldagger
Dyke	Pervert
Faggot	Feminist
Queer	Amazon
Man-hater	Sissy
Femme	Fairy
Diesel-dyke	Witch

A short discussion is sufficient here. Take a couple of the terms and talk about them. For example, show how so many terms describe not being the Norm (queer, pervert) or not fitting into role (butch, sissy, fairy, Amazon, diesel-dyke). Hold a short discussion of how roles (masculine and feminine) are used to control. And finally, point out how some of the words (faggot, witch) keep alive our memories of one of the ultimate means of control: the burning of people who are different— faggots and witches at the stake, Jews in concentration camp ovens, Blacks in their homes with crosses ablaze outside. The words are used to remind us what will happen to us if we step out of line, if we are too vocal, if we demand our rights, if we forget to be quiet, to pass, to be invisible.

III. Myths and stereotypes

Ask the group to give all the myths and stereotypes they have heard about lesbians. Here are a few:

* Lesbians like to look like men.
* Lesbians seduce children.
* Lesbians all play softball.
* All lesbians need is a good lay.
* All lesbians are either butch or femme.
* Lesbians want to do men's jobs.
* Women become lesbians because they have had bad experiences with men.
* Lesbians have had bad childhood experiences with their fathers.
* Lesbians have had bad childhood experiences with their mothers.

- Lesbians want other people's children because they can't have any of their own.
- Lesbians socialize only in dark and dirty bars.
- All lesbians are alcoholics.
- Lesbians hate themselves.
- All lesbians are strong and powerful.

You will get a long working list of these. Choose a few favorites to talk about, usually beginning with "Lesbians seduce children," because this provides an opportunity to get into a discussion of violence against women and children right away. First, ask the group who it is in the majority of cases who abuses children. Ask them to raise their hands if they have ever personally known a lesbian who sexually assaulted a child in school. Ask them if they ever knew a man who did this. Who created this myth about homosexuals when the great majority of all child sexual abuse is done by heterosexual men? And for what purpose was the myth created? (It is diversionary and helps protect the true abusers.) Make a strong statement here about the abuse of children — that we in the movement to end violence against women and children do not believe in the sexual abuse of children by *anyone.*

Next, go on to talk about "Lesbians want to do men's jobs," and once again point out that homphobia is not a system of discrimination created to control just lesbians but all women. Why are we in our organizations supposed to be so terrorized when someone says, "All of you working there are just a bunch of lesbians"? Why are we told it isn't "womanly" to do non-traditional jobs that pay higher salaries?

And finally, to end on a light note: "Women become lesbians because they have had bad experiences with men." To which I say, if that were the case, then all women would be lesbians.

IV. Invisibility Role Play

Ask for one brave woman who clearly defines herself as a non-lesbian to do this one; if you can't get a volunteer, ask the entire group to imagine along with you and then discuss it afterwards.

Here is the situation: Imagine that you as a non-lesbian are part of a group that is only ten percent of the population and your heterosexual, non-lesbian activity is illegal, and your lifestyle must be kept hidden from the public lest it reveal your sexual proclivity. Assume now that a family holiday such as Christmas has just finished, and I, your lesbian supervisor at work, ask you casually (for it means little to me) what you did over the holidays. How will you, the non-lesbian, describe the events of the holdidays without giving me any clues that you spent any part in intimate ways with members (nonrelated by blood, that is) of the opposite sex, and how will you keep me from knowing that you did anything connected with heterosexual institutions, roles, traditions? Will you change pronouns? Will you lie by omission? And how will you feel about yourself?

And now, in this switched-about world, I decide to give a January party for the office crew and ask all of you to bring your partners. Will you dare to bring the man you have lived secretly with for the past five years, thereby letting us all suspect/know you are abnormal, sick, illegal? And if you don't, what will you tell him as you leave him at home and go out as this pretended single woman that the world takes you to be? And what will you tell him when you get home that night? Once at the party, will you speak to other suspected non-lesbians or will you be afraid that being friendly with them might make people suspect *you?* And what will you do when I, your host, turn down the lights and put on slow-dance music — who will you dance with? And by what signals will you recognize the other non-lesbians there? Will you ask one of them to dance? Will that be too dangerous?

And when your male partner of five years, with whom you have no legal ties because there are none available to you, gets sick and goes to the hospital, how will you get to see him, how will you deal with his family that has all rights sanctioned by law, and how will you keep from exposing yourself in your love for him? And when he dies in that hospital and you have no right to the body, to burial, to recognition of your relationship, to public grief or support, what will you do? Where will you turn?

This role-play can be taken along many lines. I recommend that you be fairly relentless with it, pushing it until everyone in the room feels what it means to be so in fear of the loss of one's job, one's children, one's church, one's community, that a lesbian would feel forced to live a double life, to change gender pronouns, to lie about her life outside work, to keep quiet about her feelings (even when in excruciating pain about the loss/death of a partner). Push it until everyone understands the stress that lesbians live with every minute if they are closeted at all, the stress that their relationships suffer because of closeting and the absence of societal sanctions, the terrible struggle with integrity at every turn. Help non-lesbians to understand that when a lesbian is suffering from homophobic oppression and has to choose partial or complete invisibility, she feels like a six-foot person forced to walk around in a room with a five-foot ceiling.

It is absolutely essential that participants understand why so many lesbians choose invisibility as their only means of survival, even though we all know that invisibility keeps us divided from each other and unable to speak against our own oppression and keeps us from having the support of sympathetic non-lesbians. At a workshop in Pennsylvania, a non-lesbian was having trouble seeing why our sexual preference was more than a bedroom issue, why it was so dangerous, and a very fine and brave woman whom everyone there had thought to be a non-lesbian for years came out and said, "Because when I tell you that I am a lesbian, as I do at this moment, I give you the power to destroy my life."

PART TWO

Homophobia was created as a weapon to enforce male dominance and power. It is about keeping women and men bound to traditional sex roles and their inherent inequality. As long as homophobic remarks and attacks strike fear in our hearts, then homophobia is an effective means of keeping all of us in control and in the service of the few.

I. How Lesbians Are Battered Women/Why Lesbians Are in the Battered Women's Movement

It is at this point that the connection between battering, rape, incest, and homophobia is to be made. Each of these is violence against women, each is about power over women, and each is about *controlling* women. Each is not so much related to sexuality as to the use of power and control. As Bernice Reagon once said, we women all remember somewhere in our cells what happened to us in former days when we stepped out of line — we were burned as witches — and for that reason, many women are afraid to show strength and independence today. Instead of burnings, today our activity, strength and independence are kept limited by violence and the threat of violence. Lesbians are committed to work to end violence in the lives of women because we understand these connections and suffer from all of these forms of control.

Some similarities between lesbians and battered women are:

1) they risk loss of community if they tell of their experiences
2) they risk loss of their children
3) they are kept isolated and silenced
4) they are frequently blamed for their experiences and told if they would only change, then they would be accepted
5) they are sometimes physically battered.

II. Lesbian-baiting

Lesbian-baiting is a conscious action, often subtle, to get lesbians out of organizations and to control the work of women. It can take the form of firing lesbians outright on trumped-up charges, of threatening lesbians about the damage their visibility is causing the organization, and of generally making lesbians' worklives miserable by coolness, indifference, lack of support, exclusion, low pay, few rewards, no advancement. Lesbian-baiting from women within an organization usually comes from fear. When lesbian-baiting comes from the outside — "We can't in good faith refer clients to you anymore because we know there are lesbians on your staff" — it is a way of controlling all women, women's work, women's expression and freedom. How can any woman anywhere ever prove she is not a lesbian? And to what extremes does she have to go in the attempt to prove her acceptability in a male-defined world? When non-lesbian staff are confronted, they almost always speak of the good of the organization, or the best of them simply say they don't know what to do to protect both the lesbians and the organization. The problem-solving strategy sections are designed to help those who mean well and just don't know what to do.

III. Problem-solving

Break the large group up into small groups (six to eight people each) and give them one of these problems (written on a piece of paper) to talk about and solve together. Allow at least fifteen to twenty minutes, and then have each group report back to the large group.

Examples:

1) You overhear two kids calling each other "Queer" and "Faggot" in the shelter. What do you as a staff person do?

2) Before the support group starts, a resident tells a queer joke, and most women laugh. You, as group leader however, know there is a closeted lesbian in the group. What do you do?

3) A battered woman in a shelter suspects that a staff member is a lesbian and goes to the director, saying she won't stay in the same shelter with a lesbian. How do you as director handle this?

4) The child advocate at your shelter is a lesbian. Two mothers come to you and say they don't want this woman touching their children. What do you do?

5) Someone from your primary referral group calls and says he doesn't feel that he can refer any more women to the shelter because it is common knowledge around town that the shelter has lesbians on the staff. What do you as director do?

6) A lesbian separates from her lover of eight years and is despondent and distracted for weeks. Her distress is evident to everyone in the shelter. How do you deal with this with everyone in the shelter? How do you support her?

IV. Strategies

For this session, it is helpful to do brainstorming with the entire group. Deal with each essential category: battered women in the shelter, staff, volunteers, board, funders, community. Get people to seek realistic measures and to begin with small, realizable steps. For example, a seemingly small step is to begin using the word *lesbian* easily and effortlessly in talks with different groups. For instance, in a talk with the board or funders, include lesbians in the list of women you serve and hire, along with older women, women of color, etc. The reason for this small step is to rob the word of its potency. If everyone in the organization is afraid to use the word lesbian and if it isn't spoken, then it holds terrible power. Put it out in public into common acceptance, both in talks and in written work. Then the organization will be in less of a defensive place when the word lesbian is used negatively against it. Many other strategies will come from the group, but keep each concrete and reality-based.

Two important strategies to discuss:

1) how to create an antihomophobic program;
2) how to let your community know you are antihomophobic, that you support lesbians.

V. Non-lesbian Support of Lesbians

Divide into small groups again and discuss concrete ways non-lesbians can support lesbians and do antihomophobic work. Allow twenty to thirty minutes, and then report back to the large group. (Important note: In this session, and throughout the workshop, it is important not to expose invisible lesbians in the group. Be sensitive to this, and also seek ways to validate them and their work by talking about the examples for fine lesbian leadership in social change work, in women's publications and music, in the poetry of Adrienne Rich and Audre Lorde, etc. The very fact that an out lesbian is leading this workshop and that the subject of homophobia is being discussed will be validation in itself.)

And finally: This workshop is only a beginning, a piece of work waiting to be changed and improved upon, for that is the way the world is transformed, piece by piece, improvement by improvement. Its goal is to provide enough information for people to *begin* a dialogue about lesbian existence and lesbian issues in the movement. It recognizes that it is a hard, slow, and often painful journey for human rights, but that if we are to work for women, then we must recognize the importance of lesbian existence and the interconnectedness of our lives, our work, and our freedom.

Resources

Support groups, safe homes and shelter services for battered lesbians are emerging throughout the country.

For more information about the services closest to you or for more information on lesbian battering, contact:

The National Coalition Against Domestic Violence
2401 Virginia Avenue, N.W. Suite 306
Washington D.C. 20037
202/293-8860
638-6388

Contributor Notes

Mindy Benowitz is a feminist psychotherapist practicing in Minnesota. She has participated in the Task Force on Violence in Lesbian Relationships since 1982. She has also worked as an advocate in a battered women's shelter for three years, and led homophobia workshops throughout Minnesota.

Breeze: In 1980, I implemented the first domestic violence program in a Southwestern rural community. In 1982 I left all full time work to fulfill a lifelong dream of being a writer. I have just completed my first novel, a lesbian romance *(Reel to Real)* for which I am currently seeking a publisher. All of my writing focuses on the self empowerment of womyn — lesbians in particular. I am presently residing on the East Coast with a lover/writer who shares my life of spiritual enrichment in a gentle, loving relationship.

Donna Cecere is a native New Yorker, resides in Denver where she works in Pharmacy and is active in the Colorado A.I.D.S. Project. She does not ski.

Mary Lou Dietrich: I still live in a cabin in the woods with a dog. Occasionally, deer, coyotes, and humanoid friends visit us. Since my battering experience, I have started doing volunteer hotline counseling for the local battered women's shelter. I want to live in a world without war, rape, battering, lesbian-hating, and environmental destruction. I don't know what to do with my anger. I split lots of firewood. I'm looking for my sense of humor which disappeared about a year ago. Has anyone seen it?

Cory Dziggel is a sculptor, painter and potter turned activist in the battered women's movement. She is a countrywoman and the parent of a sweet and cantankerous toddler, Travis. She has identified as a lesbian since she was a teenager. She is the Program Coordinator of Berks Women in Crisis in Pennsylvania and in that work is firmly committed to the empowerment of all battered women. Perhaps her greatest joy in this work is found in nurturing children and facilitating alliances between battered women and their kids.

Cedar Gentlewind: I am a forty year old lesbian. I grew up with incest, abuse, battery and parental alcoholism. Today I support and live with my youngest son and engage in the continual process of healing and growing.

Linda Geraci first became involved in the battered women's movement as a volunteer at Womenshelter/Compañeras, in Holyoke, Massachusetts. Since then, she has volunteered at My Sister's Place in Washington, D.C., as well as for the national office of the National Coalition Against Domestic Violence. While at NCADV, she became involved in the legal and legislative issues surrounding battering. Currently, she is attending Georgetown University Law Center and intends to practice public interest law.

Linda F. Giddings is an Eastern Band Cherokee-Choctaw-Creole, forty year old, differently abled Indian Rights activist who has been an organizer in the movement to end violence against women and children for thirteen years. An incest survivor and former battered woman, Linda has co-founded (with the help of her partner of eleven years and their children) two domestic violence/sexual assault programs, including a safe home program for battered lesbians. Currently Linda is serving as the Washington State representative to the National Coalition Against Domestic Violence, on the steering committee of the Washington State Shelter Network, and as director of Evergreen Human Services, a rural domestic violence and sexual assault program.

Nancy Hammond lives in Minneapolis, Minnesota where she is a member of the Task Force on Violence in Lesbian Relationships. Since 1979 she has worked with lesbians who have been abused by their lovers, and most recently has been involved in creating both educational and support groups for battered lesbians.

Barbara Hart is an organizer and activist lawyer who has worked in the movement to end violence against women since 1971. She is staff counsel for the Pennsylvania Coalition Against Domestic Violence and an associate with the Leadership Institute for Women. She loves problem-solving and organizing for social change. She has recently authored a manual on monitoring and evaluating counseling/educational programs for men who batter. She is also the mother of the sweet and cantankerous child, Travis.

Arlene Istar: I am a Jewish, working class, physically challenged lesbian-feminist, who is also a recovering substance abuser. I work as an alcoholism counselor and healer, working especially with lesbians and womyn incest survivors. I am an active member of the Lesbian Safety Network, an Albany, New York-based group, organizing around crisis issues in the lesbian community, particularly lesbian battering. I hope to move back to the country soon, and become a mommy.

Kim: Currently, I am a student working on my degrees in Journalism and TV Broadcasting and Women's Studies. I do a weekly radio show at the university, where I address various women's issues. I enjoy writing short stories and poetry, photography, and playing the piano. Since writing my story I have completed co-dependency treatment and have just recently completed chemical dependency treatment for a second time. I plan on starting an AA group for women on our university campus. I am also making plans to reorganize our group of women to address the issue of battering between the women in our community. Continuing to reach out to others has helped me tremendously. Participating in this writing project has meant a great deal to me also. I hope this book reaches other lesbian women who have had to live with battering in their lives. It is truly a book written in response to a great need. Many thanks for allowing me to be a part of all this.

Sue Knollenberg has worked at the Minnesota Coalition for Battered Women since 1980. As a program coordinator, she coordinates legislative activities, provides technical assistance and assists in training. She has been a member of the Violence in Lesbian Relationships Task Force since its inception and has coordinated a two-part statewide training on homophobia.

Susan Kresge has returned to the Pacific Northwest — land of her mothers — and is piecing together the remnants of her past. Through movement and body work, writing, long walks along the ocean and mountain quests, she is healing old wounds and sourcing the spirits of transformation.

Marcia LaRose has been active in the women's anti-violence movement for nine years. Marcia is currently the director of the Portland Women's Crisis Line in Portland, Oregon. She is a formerly battered woman and the mother of six adult children. Marcia has six grandchildren.

Lisa: I grew up in the wastelands of Southern California, escaping to the Bay area in 1971. It has been three years now since the end of my abusive relationship. Since that time, I've been working to heal myself and figure out what I want in life. I presently live a hectic and somewhat hedonistic existence —

juggling school, work and several women in my life! In my spare time I tend to sleep.

Blair Northwood: A Colorado semi-native (here for fourteen years), I have continued my work in the battered women's movement. I co-facilitated a workshop on battered lesbians at the second NCADV National Conference in Milwaukee in 1982, and have held various positions with Colorado shelters and our statewide coalition. I recently stopped trying to save the world, and have left my counseling career to work with computers. Since the events in the article, I have learned to have positive and loving relationships. I currently live in Fort Collins with my cat Pearl and seven teddy bears.

Suzanne Pharr is an organizer in the South.

Nomi Porat has worked within the domestic violence movement for six years. She has conducted trainings on lesbian abuse and homophobia for northern California domestic violence agencies. For the past two years, she has actively participated in the Lesbian Abuse Issues Network, a lesbian group interested in exposing the extent of lesbian battering through a comprehensive Lesbian Relationship Survey and establishing accessible services to both battered lesbians and batterers. She has facilitated support groups for battered lesbians, heterosexual battered women and women in jail. She is on the San Francisco Commission on the Status of Women Fund Allocations Committee and was honored by the Western Center on Domestic Violence as a Woman of Achievement in 1986.

Linda Shaw was a co-founder of a battered women's program in Pennsylvania in the 1970s, where she developed and led support groups for both lesbian and non-lesbian battered women. She was a member of the Maryland Network Against Domestic Violence and representative to the National Coalition Against Domestic Violence from 1981-1985.

Lydia Walker lives and works in Arkansas where she acts as an advocate for battered women and children who are not living at the Project's shelter facility. She has been a political worker for gay rights and the battered women's movement for many years and is a member of both the Rural Task Force and Child Task Force of the National Coalition Against Domestic Violence. She is currently the secretary of NCADV's steering committee, and has recently begun sharing some of her writing with other women.

Maria Zavala: I'm thirty-one years old and was born in Brooklyn, New York to recent migrants from the island of Puerto Rico. I'm an incest survivor and was a physically abused child. I married when I was eighteen, was abused physically, emotionally and sexually by my husband for four years. I had one good thing come from all of that and that was my son. I left my husband ten years ago. I've worked in a shelter for battered women and their children, Womanshelter/ Compañeras in Holyoke, Massachusetts, for four years where I'm a bilingual, bicultural counselor and legal advocate. I've been on the coordinating board for the Massachusetts Coalition for Battered Women's Service Groups for four years and I've represented the state of Massachusetts to the National Coalition Against Domestic Violence for three and one half years.

About the Editor:

Kerry Lobel is a lesbian activist who has been a worker in the battered women's movement since 1976. After working for two years as an advocate for battered women and their children, Kerry served as the executive director of the Southern California Coalition on Battered Women for five years. In 1984 she moved to Little Rock, Arkansas, where she currently works as a consultant to women's programs and social change organizations throughout the United States.